Multiple-choice
questions for
Introduction
to Business
Management

Multiple-choice questions for
Introduction to Business Management

Sharon Rudansky-Kloppers & Johan Strydom

OXFORD
UNIVERSITY PRESS

SOUTHERN AFRICA

SOUTHERN AFRICA

Oxford University Press Southern Africa (Pty) Ltd

Vasco Boulevard, Goodwood, Cape Town, Republic of South Africa
P O Box 12119, N1 City, 7463, Cape Town, Republic of South Africa

Oxford University Press Southern Africa (Pty) Ltd is a subsidiary of
Oxford University Press, Great Clarendon Street, Oxford OX2 6DP.

The Press, a department of the University of Oxford, furthers the University's objective of
excellence in research, scholarship, and education by publishing worldwide in

Oxford New York

Auckland Cape Town Dar es Salaam Hong Kong Karachi
Kuala Lumpur Madrid Melbourne Mexico City Nairobi
New Delhi Shanghai Taipei Toronto

With offices in

Argentina Austria Brazil Chile Czech Republic France Greece
Guatemala Hungary Italy Japan Poland Portugal Singapore South Korea
Switzerland Turkey Ukraine Vietnam

Oxford is a registered trade mark of Oxford University Press
in the UK and in certain other countries

Published in South Africa
by Oxford University Press Southern Africa (Pty) Ltd, Cape Town

Multiple-choice Questions for Introduction to Business Management
ISBN 978 019 905040 6

© Oxford University Press Southern Africa (Pty) Ltd 2010

The moral rights of the author have been asserted
Database right Oxford University Press Southern Africa (Pty) Ltd (maker)

First published 2010
3rd impression 2011

Publisher/Commissioning editor: Alida Terblanche
Editor: Nicola van Rhyn
Designer: Jade Benjamin
Cover designer: Samantha Rowles

Set in 10 pt on 12 pt Photina by Elbert Visser
Printed and bound by Clyson Printers, Maitland, Cape Town
SW4771

Acknowledgements
The authors and publisher gratefully acknowledge permission to reproduce copyright material in this
book. Every effort has been made to trace copyright holders, but if any copyright
infringements have been made, the publisher would be grateful for information that would
enable any omissions or errors to be corrected in subsequent impressions.

9780406108601

Table of contents

Preface

The format of the book

The book consists of 15 chapters that cover different aspects of business management. Chapters 1 to 4 deal with the business world and place of business management, while chapters 5 to 9 deal with general management principles. Chapters 10 to 14 cover the functional areas of a business and the last chapter deals with the strategic management process.

Each chapter starts off with a brief description of the management aspect dealt with. All chapters, except Chapter 15, cover 20 multiple-choice questions which range from easy to moderate to challenging. The questions test both theory and practice and have been chosen to cover a wide range within each subject area.

All questions have been pre-tested. Some questions assess lower level skills of knowledge, while others are designed to test higher level skills of application, analysis and evaluation. The answers to the first five questions of each chapter are provided at the end of the chapter. The rest of the answers can be obtained by visiting the following website: http://www.oxford.co.za/mcq/users/register. Here you can register to have access to the answers by using the unique code that you will find on the imprint page of your copy of the book.

The book is useful in preparing students for multiple-choice examinations and will help students with both their understanding of business management and their examination performance.

Answering multiple-choice questions

For most of the multiple-choice questions in the book, the single correct answer is either 1, 2, 3, 4 or 5. Students should decide on each alternative independently.

When answering a multiple-choice question, a good deal of time is often wasted (especially in the examination) by reading all four alternatives before deciding which is the correct one. The secret is to read and decide on each alternative separately. For example, if the question asks you to identify which statement is correct, take a ruler and cover the other three statements so that you only see the first statement. Read it and then, without reading any other statement, decide whether the statement is correct, wrong or you don't know. Put a tick next to it if you think it is correct; put a cross next to it if you think it is wrong; and put a ? if you are not sure. Then move the ruler down so that you can read the second statement. Again decide and mark the category in which it falls.

When you have done that with every one of the four statements, you may find that you have marked one statement correct and three statements wrong. That is then your answer. If you find that you have marked two correct, then compare the two statements and choose the one that seems to be the most correct, or the most comprehensive.

When you have selected your answer for a particular question, it is essential that you write down your reasons for doing so. For example, if you chose alternative 2 as the correct answer, you should write on a separate sheet of paper why you think it is correct. Write down the actual reference in the prescribed book on which you base your reasoning. However, you must even go a step further. You must also write down why the other alternatives are wrong. Again make specific reference to the prescribed book to back up your reasoning.

Students should understand the subject matter and be able to explain the concepts and apply the principles. That is why it is so important for you to be able to give a reason for your answer.

Contributors

Content editors:
Sharon Rudansky-Kloppers
Johan Strydom

Authors:
Natasha Da Silva-Esclana
Nadine Lenhard
Tracey Cohen
Petri Prinsloo
Petro Coetzee

The business world and business management

Business plays a vital role in the survival of society. Businesses need to ensure the optimal use of available resources in order to thrive and satisfy society's needs. Businesses operate within a larger economic system and these systems include:

- socialism
- market economy
- command economy.

MULTIPLE-CHOICE QUESTIONS

Easy questions

1   The **primary** task of business management is to ...
    1   provide solutions for the management problems experienced in business enterprises
    2   study the economic needs that have to be satisfied in the community
    3   examine the factors in the macro-environment which influence the activities in the micro-environment
    4   determine how an enterprise can achieve the highest possible output with the least possible input.

2   A business's effort to provide the greatest possible **need satisfaction** with limited available resources is known as ...
    1   need satisfaction
    2   productivity
    3   rate of return on total capital
    4   the economic principle.

3   Which of the following is a **disadvantage** of socialism?
    1   Socialism is an unstable environment
    2   Socialism has cyclical fluctuations
    3   Socialism results in a low standard of living
    4   State organisations are unproductive.

4   Within the **free-market** economy, the state or government's interference in the economic system is limited to ...
    1   a maximum
    2   within reason
    3   a minimum.

5   The .... function creates a **favourable image** of the business and it promotes goodwill between the business and the external groups that are directly and indirectly involved in the business.
    1   production and operations
    2   purchasing
    3   marketing
    4   public relations.

Moderate questions

6   Circle the following statements that are **correct**?
    a   Profit is the driving force behind entrepreneurs and their businesses in a free market
    b   Individuals can own land, factories and equipment under the command economy
    c   In the socialist economy, the state can stabilise economic fluctuations
    d   Within the free-market economy, the economic environment is unstable.
    1   a, b, c
    2   b, c, d

3 a, c, d

4 a, b, d

7 Which **one** of the following statements regarding **socialism** is true?
1 Farmers, factory owners, industrialists and individuals are free to do what they want with their assets
2 The state owns and controls the community's resources
3 The state owns and controls principle industries such as transportation, health services and energy
4 There is minimum state interference in markets.

8 Which **one** of the following statements is **correct**?
1 In socialism, the state controls the most important industries and resources
2 The state plays no role in a free-market economy
3 In a free-market economy, business organisations may not exploit the consumer
4 In socialism, the state owns all the business organisations.

9 Thabo is an entrepreneur. He knows that there are risks involved in starting a new business and that he has to satisfy the unlimited needs of his community when he opens his Sebenza Spaza shop. Thabo now wonders about the limited resources he has at his disposal. Which of the following is an **example of capital** that Thabo will need to have available in order to facilitate opening the Sebenza Spaza shop?
1 Gladys, Thabo's friend, will make her bookkeeping skills available to Thabo once he opens Sebenza Spaza shop
2 The cash register and building that Thabo intends to rent from a company called Spaza Direct
3 The residential site where Thabo wants to open the Sebenza Spaza shop

4 Sibusiso is Thabo's partner in the Sebenza Spaza shop.

10 Nomsa has just completed her degree in Business Management at Unisa. She is quite keen to start her own business where she will sell cupcakes online, packaging them in beautiful boxes with ribbons on them. She registered her business under the name Sparkle Cupcakes and is planning to purchase a small car that she will use to deliver the cupcakes. She has also secured a contract with a supplier, EasyBake, that will provide her with high quality ingredients such as baking powder and icing at low prices. Which one of the following statements is **correct**?
1 The icing and baking powder provided by EasyBake is considered to be a production factor for EasyBake
2 The small car that Nomsa purchased from AutoDirect is part of the final product provided by Sparkle Cupcakes
3 The boxes and ribbons used by Sparkle Cupcakes are used as a production factor and contribute towards the end product
4 The boxes and ribbons used to package the cupcakes are the end product that Sparkle Cupcakes will sell.

11 Which of the following statements on the **state and economic systems** are **correct**?
a State intervention to solve an economic problem in a free-market economy indicates a move towards a command or centrally-controlled economy
b Government intervention in the economic system aims at encouraging economic growth and stability
c Control of strategic organisations cannot be left to profit-seeking entrepreneurs
d An expanding entrepreneurial role

by the state eventually leads to a democracy.

1 a, c
2 b, c
3 a, b, d
4 a, b, c, d

12 There are several economic systems in the world. The country of Utopia allows and encourages all members of the community to possess houses and to earn profits on them by renting the houses out to overseas tourists. Clothing and food are allocated based on free market demand and are not controlled by the government. All residents of Utopia are allowed to choose which careers they want to follow. Indicate which **economic system** Utopia uses?

1 free-market
2 command economy
3 socialism
4 communism.

Challenging questions

13 As an economic system, a **free-market economy** is characterised by which of the following attributes?

a private ownership of production factors
b free competition
c profit motive recognised
d limited right to strike in state enterprises.

1 a, b
2 b, d
3 a, b, c
4 a, b, c, d

14 Which of the following statements are **correct**?

a The need for self-esteem mainly affects people who have already satisfied their lower order needs
b Basic physical and psychological needs may overlap
c A person will first satisfy some of his/her security needs before he/she

satisfies his/her survival needs
d Self-realisation needs are lower order needs.

1 a, c
2 b, c, d
3 c, d
4 a, b

15 Which of the following statements on the **economic principle** are correct?

a Ensuring the highest possible satisfaction of needs with scarce resources is known as the economic principle
b The economic principle refers to a business's endeavour to keep its input costs as high as possible
c Businesses that apply the economic principle try to achieve the highest possible income
d The economic system is not subject to the economic principle.

1 a
2 a, c, d
3 b, c, d
4 c, d

16 Which of the following statements are **correct**?

a Mary's need for self-esteem will only be satisfied once her lower order needs have been met
b Anne's need for love and recognition will be satisfied before she satisfies her self-realisation needs
c John will first satisfy some of his security needs before he satisfies his survival needs
d Self-realisation needs are lower order needs.

1 a, b
2 c, d
3 a, b, d
4 b, c, d

17 As an economic system, a **command economy** is characterised by which of the following attributes?

a basic industries owned by the state
b profit motive recognised
c management environment is the state
d low productivity.
   1 a, b
   2 c, d
   3 b, c, d
   4 a, b, c, d

18 The world is divided into three basic **economic systems** and each system has its own unique **characteristics**. Match the correct characteristic in Block B with the appropriate economic system in Block A.

BLOCK A
Economic system
a   Free market
b   Command economy
c   Socialism

BLOCK B
Characteristic
(i)   Generally has low productivity and increases the difficulty of proper planning
(ii)   The main driving force in the market is profit generation
(iii) The state has full control over production factors thereby increasing competition in the market
(iv)   Employees are free to choose employment and have a limited right in government institutions to participate in strikes

1 a (ii)   b (i)   c (iv)
2 a (iv)   b (i)   c (iii)
3 a (iv)   b (iii)   c (ii)
4 a (ii)   b (iii)   c (i)

19 Match the functional areas in business management in Block A with the description in Block B.

BLOCK A
Functional areas
a   Marketing function
b   Financial function
c   Purchasing function
d   Production and operations function

BLOCK B
Description
(i)   Acquisition of all products and materials required by the business to function profitably
(ii)   Creates a favourable image of the business and it promotes goodwill between the business and the external groups that are directly and indirectly involved in the business
(iii) Assessment of the market and the needs of customers
(iv)   Establishment and layout of the production unit and the conversion from raw material into finished goods
(v)   Ensures the maximum profitability of the business, without the danger of insolvency or liquidation

1 a (i)   b (ii)   c (iii)   d (iv)
2 a (ii)   b (i)   c (v)   d (iii)
3 a (iii)   b (v)   c (i)   d (iv)
4 a (iv)   b (ii)   c (iii)   d (v)

20 Within the **free-market economy** ...... and ...... is true.
1 free competition; high social costs
2 free competition; limited choice of a job
3 no profit is allowed; limited right to strike
4 no profit is allowed; low productivity.

SUGGESTED SOLUTIONS
TO THE FIRST FIVE QUESTIONS

Q	A
1	4
2	4
3	4
4	3
5	4

Entrepreneurship

Entrepreneurship is seen as the driving force within any organisation. Entrepreneurs play a vital role in the small business industry and the economy at large. They also follow the entrepreneurial process in order to determine whether their ideas are viable business opportunities. Entrepreneurs have a number of skills, characteristics and resources that are important for them to be successful in the business world.

MULTIPLE-CHOICE QUESTIONS

Easy questions

1 **Small and medium enterprises** in South Africa are defined as ...
   1 having less than 200 employees, an annual turnover of less than R100 000 and direct managerial involvement by the owners
   2 having less than 50 employees, an annual turnover of less than R64 million and direct managerial involvement of the owners
   3 having less than 200 employees, an annual turnover of less than R64 million and direct managerial involvement
   4 having less than 200 employees, an annual turnover of less than R64 million and capital assets of more than R10 million.

2 Jack developed an idea to start a laundromat. During the .... stage of the **entrepreneurial process,** Jack thoroughly researched his idea and collected data to help him forecast whether his idea and venture would survive.
   1 feasibility study
   2 opportunity identification
   3 market analysis
   4 business planning.

3 Peter intends opening a cellphone repair business in his rural community. He is currently busy collecting information from the villagers that will help him establish whether the idea will work or not. This information includes how many people in the area own cellphones and how often they require repair services for their cellphones.
   Make a mark to indicate the correct **business term** for the activity Peter is currently undertaking?
   1 business study
   2 feasibility study
   3 business planning
   4 viability study.

4 The **ability** to consider what the future might offer, how this impacts on the business, and what needs to be done now to prepare for it is called ...
   1 strategy skills
   2 marketing skills
   3 planning skills
   4 project management skills.

5 Within a **franchise,** the franchisor is the entrepreneur and the franchisee is the intrapreneur.
   1 true
   2 false.

Moderate questions

6   Circle the following **skills** that are required to be a successful entrepreneur:
  a strategy skills
  b marketing skills
  c financial skills
  d project management skills
  e human relations skills
  f planning skills
  g organising skills
  h motivation skills
  i control skills.
    1 a, b, c, d, e, f
    2 a, b, c, d, e, i
    3 a, c, f, g, h, i
    4 a, b, c, e, f, i

7   Which of the following statements are **correct**?
    An **entrepreneur** is someone who ...
  a pursues profit
  b accepts risk
  c makes the most of opportunities in the environment
  d combines expertise and resources to provide products and services.
    1 a, b
    2 a, b, c, d
    3 a, c, d
    4 b, c, d

8   Which of the following statements are **advantages** of buying an existing business?
  a The business already has experienced employees
  b The supplier relations are already in place
  c The inventory and equipment are in place
  d The employees are inherited rather than chosen.
    1 a, b
    2 a, b, c
    3 a, c, d
    4 a, b, c, d

9   Which of the following statements about **franchising** are correct?
  a Franchisees have the freedom to experiment, operate and market their business based on their own vision
  b Franchisees must usually strictly adhere to the franchisor's plans
  c Franchisors usually fall in the medium-sized to large business category
  d The franchisor is an entrepreneur.
    1 a, b, c, d
    2 b, c, d
    3 a, b, c
    4 a, d

10 Which of the following characteristics of a **small or medium** enterprise are correct?
  a must be listed on the Johannesburg Stock Exchange (JSE)
  b have fewer than 200 employees
  c have an annual turnover of less than R64 million
  d have capital assets of less than R10 million.
    1 c, d
    2 b, c, d
    3 a, b, c
    4 a, b, c, d

11 Entrepreneurs are often faced with the choice of whether to start a new business or buy an existing business. Which of the following are **advantages** associated with buying an **existing business**?
  a supplier relations are in place
  b employees are inherited rather than chosen
  c planning can be based on historical data
  d possible owner financing.
    1 a, b
    2 b, d
    3 a, b, c
    4 a, c, d

12 Ayanda is an entrepreneur. She owns an enterprise called Kiddie Cooks. Kiddie Cooks provides children's cooking classes. Ayanda decided to open her business after several years of experience at a chef training centre in Centurion. Ayanda provides children and their parents the opportunity to work together in her studio kitchen. It is here that children will learn different cooking skills. In her classes children will learn the basics of cooking, using the right utensils and following a recipe. Children learn to have patience, perseverance and to follow-through with a project to get to an end result. Ayanda has put in long hours in the planning and developing of Kiddie Cooks. In order to get the business started Ayanda used her own assets as surety for financing. She knows that it was a risky move and that she stands to lose her assets should Kiddie Cooks not be successful. However, Kiddie Cooks has been so successful that Ayanda now arranges children's parties around a cooking theme in her studio kitchen. She is so busy that she had to employ an assistant and a cleaning lady.

Ayanda has worked single-mindedly towards her goal to own her own enterprise focusing on children cooking. Ayanda is ambitious and has a competitive nature. She has always been attracted to jobs that challenge her skills and problem-solving abilities. Which **trait** is being described?
1 achievement motivation
2 internal locus of control
3 innovation and creativity
4 risk taking.

Challenging questions
13 Which of the following can be considered an **entrepreneurial activity**?
1 Lucy has started her own cleaning business following a request from a local insurance firm to take over their cleaning

2 Sam wants to learn how to do professional photography and applies for a position at the local photography shop
3 Kabelo is afraid of working at a high-risk firm and asks for a demotion
4 Caron is tired of being driven to perform at the hotel where she works and decides to run her mother's guesthouse.

Read the following brief scenario and answer question 14 that follows:

Nathan and his wife love cats. So much so that they have rescued and housed seven cats in their neighbourhood. When owners are away, cats start to wander the streets of Nathan's neighbourhood and might become startled and lost. Nathan realised that looking after cats might be a wonderful business opportunity. He considered opening a cat hotel. He spoke to a number of cat owners in his neighbourhood and found that they would consider leaving their cats in a facility where they would be looked after and nurtured during the holiday periods, setting the owners' minds at ease on the safety of their cats. Nathan had to follow the entrepreneurial process in order to reach the implementation and launch of his idea.

14 Put the following steps of the **entrepreneurial process** in order for Nathan's Cat Hotel.
a Nathan had to assess the opportunity of the Cat Hotel and determine whether it was a feasible idea or not
b Nathan had to compile a business plan in order to obtain finance from the bank
c Nathan had to launch Nathan's Cat Hotel and manage the new business
d Nathan had to clarify whether he and his wife have all the abilities and skills it takes to start Nathan's Cat Hotel
e Beside capital, Nathan had to determine whether they have time, energy and other resources in order to launch Nathan's Cat Hotel.

1 a, b, c, d, e
2 b, c, d, e, a
3 e, c, d, b, a
4 d, e, a, b, c
5 c, b, d, a, e

15 Match the concept in Block A with the explanation in Block B.

BLOCK A	
a	Entrepreneurship
b	Capital
c	Natural resources
d	Human resources
e	Management

BLOCK B	
(i)	Starting your own business
(ii)	Borrowing R100 000 from ABSA
(iii)	Having a borehole on the farm so that you can irrigate your own vegetables
(iv)	Acquiring a BCom degree
(v)	Making decisions such as planning, organising, leading and control

1 a (v)   b (ii)   c (iii)   d (iv)   e (i)
2 a (i)   b (ii)   c (iii)   d (v)   e (iv)
3 a (i)   b (ii)   c (iii)   d (iv)   e (v)
4 a (ii)   b (i)   c (iv)   d (v)   e (iii)
5 a (iii)   b (ii)   c (iv)   d (v)   e (i)

16 Private investors did not like Jack's idea for a laundromat. As a result, he sought to obtain the R100 000 capital he needed from a bank rather than private investors. In considering his application for finance, the bank would consider the 'four Cs'.

Indicate which of the following are included in the **four Cs** that banks generally consider when evaluating a loan application.
a collateral
b capacity
c capital
d cash flow.
1 a, b
2 a, c
3 a, b, c
4 a, b, c, d

Read the case study below and answer Questions 17 and 18 that follow.

Thabang's entrepreneurial spirit

Mrs Thabang Molefi, a qualified traditional medical practitioner and beauty therapist, opened the first health spa in Soweto six years ago. Today she owns the Roots Healthcare Centre, a business with a multi-million rand turnover and branches in three South African provinces and a neighbouring country.

Since the success of the first centre in Soweto, she has grown her business considerably to establish another seven health-care centers in previously disadvantaged areas in Gauteng, KwaZulu-Natal, the Free State and a mobile unit visiting communities in rural and remote areas in the rest of the country. The Roots Healthcare concept was conceived whilst Thabang was training in London to become a beauty therapist and later in managing a spa on a luxury cruise liner. She gained invaluable practical experience and knew that Africa was calling her.

She returned with the idea of opening a health centre in Soweto, capitalising on the return to more natural and ethnic ways of living and to bring the professional healing powers of herbs to communities in townships and to share her knowledge and experience with her community at home. Her efforts to get a bank loan to open an up-market spa in Soweto failed but this was no deterrent. She opened on a smaller scale with the little personal funds she had available. In reaching out to residents of Soweto she also realised that there was a huge need for affordable health care. Western medicine was out of reach to a large section of the black population and the previously disadvantaged because of high cost.

The first two years of starting the Roots Health Care centres were difficult. In the first six months after opening her first health clinic, she paid staff salaries from her savings. She also spent a lot of time giving free talks at schools and churches in a bid to educate the people in Soweto about health care. She has created 41 jobs for women in these communities and developed some to managerial positions to run the health centres. Thabang has also outsourced services such as accounting, laundry and security to local businesses. It is her intention to branch out into franchising creating more business and job opportunities.

Source: Adele Gouws, Shoprite Checkers Woman of the Year. Available: http://www.womanoftheyear.co.za/pages/79568134/Awards-2008/Winners/Business-Entrepeneurs-Winner.asp [Last accessed 12 July 2010]

17 Which of the following **skills** did Thabang have which allowed her to make a success of the Roots Healthcare Centre?

a She positioned the centre as a unique enterprise that incorporated traditional healing into the spa experience

b She managed to run the centre in such a way that the enterprise was able to grow and expand

c She identified previously disadvantaged communities as members of society who lack proper medical access

d She was able to manage her own savings in such a way that she was able to grow the centre and pay staff salaries

e She created 41 jobs and created managerial positions for her staff.

   1 a, b, c
   2 d, c, a
   3 None of the above are skills
   4 All of the above are skills

18 The decision to start one's own enterprise should be followed by the **entrepreneurial process.** Indicate the correct sequence Thabang would have followed after she decided to start the centre.

a Thabang looked at the feasibility of the centre by chatting to friends to determine if there was a need for this kind of establishment

b Thabang realised that she lacked certain skills and then completed a course in beauty therapy as well as spa management and was able to identify a target market that has not been serviced before

c Thabang drew up a complete business plan after the bank turned down her application for a loan

d Thabang decided that she did not want to continue to work on the cruise ship, but rather to return to South Africa to start her own business

e After taking stock of what she had available to her, Thabang determined that she had enough personal savings to start the centre without a loan from the bank.

   1 a, c, e, d, b
   2 d, b, e, a, c
   3 a, b, d, c, e
   4 d, c, e, a, b

Read the brief scenario below and answer question 19 that follows:

Naledi is an entrepreneur. She purchases organic fresh produce and makes home made baby meals for daycare facilities in her community. Naledi's business is called Mama's Kitchen. Naledi has sensed that there is a definite need for such a service in her community. The daycare facilities are so filled with children that the labour cost for these facilities to produce their own wholesome meals is just too vast. Naledi needs to be in charge of her own destiny. She knows that in order for her to be successful, she can not rely on luck and fortune; she has to work hard and take responsibility for her own actions. In order for Mama's Kitchen to be successful, Naledi needs to have certain managerial skills at hand.

19 Help Naledi to fit the management skills in Block A with the correct description in Block B.

BLOCK A
MANAGERIAL SKILLS
a   Strategy skill
b   Planning skill
c   Marketing skill
d   Project management skill

BLOCK B
Description
(i)   Determining the needs of the daycare facilities, how to satisfy their needs and building a relationship with each daycare facility
(ii)   The ability to organise, set specific goals and draw schedules to ensure that the fresh produce is available at the right place and the right time
(iii)   The ability to keep track of expenditure, monitor cash flow and assess investments
(iv)   The ability to consider what the future might offer Mama's Kitchen and what needs to be done now to prepare for it
(v)   The ability to deal with people, leadership and motivation
(vi)   The ability to consider Mama's Kitchen as a whole and to understand how it fits within the market place

1 a (i)   b (ii)   c (v)   d (iv)
2 a (ii)   b (iv)   c (v)   d (iii)
3 a (v)   b (ii)   c (iii)   d (i)
4 a (vi)   b (iv)   c (i)   d (ii)

20 Which of the following statements describe corporate entrepreneurship the best?
   1 Corporate entrepreneurship occurs in an existing business when a new and diversified product is added to the current business
   2 Corporate entrepreneurship occurs when an entrepreneur working in the corporate world, establishes his own business separate from his current job
   3 Corporate entrepreneurship occurs when an entrepreneur starts his own corporate business venture
   4 Corporate entrepreneurship occurs when a corporate company hires an entrepreneur.

SUGGESTED SOLUTIONS TO THE FIRST FIVE QUESTIONS

Q	A
1	3
2	1
3	2
4	3
5	1

Establishing a business

There are various forms of enterprises that can be selected when starting a business. Various factors need to be taken into account when selecting the appropriate form of enterprise.
Each form has its own characteristics that hold certain advantages and disadvantages for the business.

The different forms of enterprises are:
- sole proprietorship
- partnership
- close cooperation
- company
- business trust.

MULTIPLE-CHOICE QUESTIONS

Easy questions

1 A **business plan** is important for the entrepreneur for which of the following reasons?
   a it forces him to arrange his/her ideas in a logical order
   b it forces him/her to simulate reality
   c it is not an essential aid when applying for financial aid.
      1 a, b, c
      2 a, b
      3 b, c
      4 a, c

2 Identify the important **location factors** when choosing a location.
   a the form of the enterprise
   b the central government policy
   c the climate
   d the social environment.
      1 a, b, c
      2 a, b, c, d
      3 a, c, d
      4 b, c, d

3 Which one of the following statements is **true**?
   1 If a member of a close corporation dies, the close corporation ceases to exist
   2 The close corporation has better capital acquisition potential than a company
   3 The partnership has many minimal legal requirements imposed by the government
   4 The partners in a partnership have limited liability.

4 Which one of the following represents the **most important** objective of a business plan?
   1 It presents a written plan on how the entrepreneur plans to exploit an opportunity
   2 It provides a way to identify the key variables that will impact on the success of the business
   3 It identifies and describes the nature of the business opportunity or new venture
   4 It acts as a management instrument for comparing actual results with planned outcomes.

5   Which one of the following is **not** a characteristic of a private company?
    1   the number of shareholders is limited to 50 people
    2   members of the general public may apply for shares in the company
    3   there must be at least one director
    4   the transferability of shares in the company is limited.

Moderate questions

6   Which two of the following represent differences between a **company** and a **close corporation**?
    a   tax liability
    b   legal requirements
    c   legal personality
    d   division between control and ownership.
        1   a, c
        2   a, d
        3   b, c
        4   b, d

7   Which of the following are characteristics of a **private company**?
    a   the number of shareholders is limited to 50 people
    b   members of the general public may apply for shares in the company
    c   the name of a private company has to end with the words (Pty) Ltd
    d   the transferability of shares in the company is limited.
        1   a, b, c, d
        2   a, b, d
        3   a, c, d
        4   b, c, d

8   Which of the following represents similarities between a **sole proprietorship** and a **partnership**?
    a   continuity of existence
    b   possibility of acquiring capital
    c   liability of the owners
    d   tax liability.
        1   a, b, c
        2   a, b, d

        3   a, c, d
        4   b, c, d
        5   a, b, c, d

9   Which **location factor** will assume priority for a newspaper publishing company?
    1   proximity to the market
    2   proximity to suppliers
    3   proximity to raw materials
    4   proximity to railroad facilities.

10 Which of the following considerations are important in choosing a **legal form** for a proposed business?
    a   degree of direct control and authority which the proprietors must have over the activities and assets of the business
    b   ratio of liquidity which the business must maintain when in operation
    c   possibilities of acquiring capital for the business upon establishment and for later expansion
    d   possibility for the transfer of ownership in the business
    e   legal requirements concerning the establishment and dissolution of the business.
        1   a, d
        2   b, e
        3   a, b, d
        4   a, c, d, e

11 The bank was impressed with Peter's application for finance and business plan, however they suggested that he first register his business as a private company. **Registering his company** in South Africa means that Peter will have to adhere to ... legal prescriptions and he will incur ... costs in the process.
    1   many; minimal
    2   few; minimal
    3   many; considerable
    4   few; considerable.

12 Mr Samuel owns JP Clothing Manufacturers. In 2009 he decided to sell
20 000 shares of his business to 30 of
his employees. Mr Samuel assures his
employees that they are only liable for
the amount that they have invested in
his business. He also informed them that
the business will now be known as JP
and Associates Clothing (PTY) Ltd. The
new form of ownership at JP Clothing is
a ...
1 partnership
2 close corporation
3 private company
4 public company.

Challenging questions

13 Sophie decided to start her own wedding
dress shop. She will be able to design,
make and tailor exclusive gowns for traditional wedding ceremonies. She would
like to have a shop in Pietermaritzburg's
central area but is not sure about the
location. She has asked you, her business advisor, to assist her with this selection. What **factors** would you take into
consideration when deciding on the
location of her shop?
a The material she would use is produced in the rural area just outside of
Pietermaritzburg
b Pietermaritzburg's climate is hot and
humid with high rain fall
c Sophie would be able to make use of
the ladies in the surrounding areas
who have innate knowledge of the
customs and designs of traditional
wedding gowns
d Pietermaritzburg is on the route to
major cities such as Durban and
transport is relatively inexpensive
when she has to deliver the gowns
across South Africa
e Pietermaritzburg's central government policy does not differ from the
policy applied across South Africa.

1 a, b, c, d, e
2 a, b, c
3 b, c, d, e
4 a, c, d

14 Tebogo is a sole proprietor for his dry
cleaning shop named Dry Wonder
in Gugulethu in the Western Cape.
Indicate which one of the following
aspects about a **sole proprietorship** is
correct.
1 The lifespan of Dry Wonder is linked
to Tebogo's legal capacity
2 Dry Wonder is a juristic person with
its own rights, assets and liabilities
3 Dry Wonder is a separate taxpayer
and liable for tax at a fixed rate
4 Ownership of Dry Wonder is trans-
ferred through the unlimited and free
transfer of shares.

15 Tebogo decides, after a couple of years,
to change the ownership of Dry Wonder
dry cleaning from a sole proprietorship
to a **close corporation**. Tebogo's brother,
Sibusiso, and their cousin, Sepati, each
buy a 30% interest in Dry Wonder.
Which of the following aspects are relevant to Dry Wonder CC?
1 The transfer of ownership to Sibusiso
and Sepati takes place by means of
the unlimited and free transfer of
shares
2 The main objective of Dry Wonder
CC is set out in the memorandum of
association
3 The association agreement states
that Tebogo and Sepati will manage
Dry Wonder CC
4 Tebogo, Sibusiso and Sepati are all
jointly liable for all claims against Dry
Wonder CC.

16 Match the **legal form** of a business in
Block A with the corresponding characteristic in Block B.

BLOCK A
Form of ownership
a   Sole proprietorship
b   Close corporation
c   Private company

BLOCK B
Characteristic
(i)   Created by the registration of a founding statement
(ii)   Owner personally liable for the debts of the business
(iii) Must have at least one director

1 a (i)   b (ii)   c (iii)
2 a (ii)   b (i)   c (iii)
3 a (iii) b (i)   c (ii)
4 a (iii) b (ii)   c (i)

17 Izel Jooste recently decided on a form of ownership for the preschool business she intends to start in Pretoria. The form of ownership she has chosen means that her business will have a separate legal personality and will be created by the registration of a founding statement.

    The **type of business** chosen by Izel is known as a ...
1 close corporation
2 partnership
3 section 21 company
4 private company.

18 In deciding on a **location** for her pre-school, which of the following factors would Izel have to consider:
a the sources of raw material
b the availability of labour
c the proximity of the market
d the availability of transport facilities.

1 a, b, c
2 a, b, d
3 b, c, d
4 a, b, c, d

19 Nathan owns a cat hotel where owners can leave their cats during the holiday periods. Nathan decides to register the cat hotel as a **close corporation (CC)**. Circle the statements that are true.
a Nathan and his wife are personally liable for the debts incurred by the cat hotel
b The cat hotel will have certain fundamental rights as set out in the country's Constitution
c The cat hotel is seen by SARS (the South African Revenue Service) as a separate taxpayer
d Julia (Nathan's wife) can transfer her interest in the cat hotel to their daughter Jennifer
e The main objective of the cat hotel is set out in a memorandum of association.
1 a, b, c
2 b, d, e
3 a, c, e
4 b, c, d

20 Sophie decides to register her business as a legal business entity. Her friend, Alice, is going to be her business partner and will contribute 50% of the capital that they will require to get the business started. However, neither Sophie nor Alice wants to take personal liability for the business, nor do they want to appoint a director. What **type of legal entity** would you suggest she register for?
1 sole proprietorship
2 partnership
3 close corporation
4 company.

SUGGESTED SOLUTIONS
TO THE FIRST FIVE QUESTIONS

Q	A
1	2
2	4
3	3
4	3
5	2

The business environment

All organisations are subject to environmental change and as the organisation forms an integral part of this environment, it is important to monitor these changes. The business environment can therefore be seen as all the factors or variables that may influence the continued and successful existence of the business organisation. The business environment is composed of three sub-environments:

- the micro-environment
- the market environment
- the macro-environment.

MULTIPLE-CHOICE QUESTIONS

Easy questions

1 The **market or task environment** consists of which of the following components?
   a competitors
   b suppliers
   c the state
   d technological environment
   e intermediaries.
      1 a, b, d
      2 a, b, e
      3 b, d, e
      4 a, b, c, e

2 Which **one** of the following factors is **not part** of a business's micro-environment?
   1 competitive strategy
   2 enterprise resources
   3 marketing opportunities
   4 public relations policy.

3 The most elementary form of **environmental scanning** involves ...
   1 the collection of primary information or special investigations
   2 the establishment of a scanning unit
   3 the use of industrial analysts to make market forecasts

4 the collection and updating of secondary information.

4 Which of the following features characterise the **typical** business environment?
   a complexity of the environment
   b increasing instability
   c environmental variables not inter-related
   d environmental uncertainty.
      1 a, b
      2 b, c, d
      3 a, b, d
      4 a, b, c, d

5 Which **one** of the following statements on the **economic environment** is wrong?
   1 The economic growth rate indirectly affects the income of the consumers of products and services
   2 The higher the growth rate is, the higher the standard of living of the population will be
   3 The high growth rate of the South African population dilutes the incomes of consumers
   4 A poor economic growth rate causes the impoverishment of consumers.

Moderate questions

6   ABC Engineering Works (Pty) Ltd lost one of its highly skilled engineers to XYZ Engineering Works Ltd because he was dissatisfied with his salary and therefore applied for another job. This event was caused by factors in ABC's .... **environment**.
1   micro
2   market
3   economic
4   macro.

7   Which of the following are examples of variables in the macro-environment?
a   the dramatic increase in bank interest rates having a negative impact on the disposable income of consumers
b   the dramatic increase in the fuel price and the knock-on effect on the prices of food and other commodities
c   the impact of HIV/Aids on the workplace and on employees
d   the involvement of multiple stakeholders in policy and programme development for the organisation.
1   a, b
2   a, b, c
3   b, c, d
4   a, b, c, d

8   Which one of the following is part of the **task environment** of a small fuel company in South Africa?
1   the development of a new synthetic fuel by Sasol
2   the allocation of state funds for multi-national corporations
3   the company's decision to reduce its inventory levels
4   the privatisation of Iscor which manufactures steel products

9   Which of the following statements are **correct**?
In the **market environment** ...

a   The buying power of a consumer refers to his or her total income
b   The consumer market embraces only durable and semi-durable products
c   Competition serves to curb excessive profits
d   Suppliers provide material, capital and labour to the business.
1   a, c, d
2   c, d
3   a, b, c
4   b, d

10 The **nature and intensity** of competition in a particular industry is determined by which of the following factors?
a   the threat of new entrants
b   the bargaining power of buyers
c   the threat of substitute products or services
d   the bargaining power of suppliers
e   the number of existing competitors.
1   a, b, c, e
2   a, b, d
3   b, c, d, e
4   a, b, c, d, e

11 Which of the following statements are correct?
Environmental scanning is necessary ...
a   to keep abreast of change
b   to determine which factors pose threats to existing goals
c   to determine which factors represent opportunities to promote current goals
d   because businesses that scan the environment systematically are more successful than those that do not.
1   a, b
2   a, b, d
3   a, b, c, d
4   c, d
5   b, c, d

12 Consider the following diagram and then answer question 12 that follows.

The various **sub-environments** within the management environment influence each other in different ways. In the diagram above, (b) represents ... while (d) represents ...

1 influence on consumers through strategy; direct influence through economic policies and social variables
2 influence on consumers through strategy; direct influence by competitors
3 direct influence by competitors; indirect influence through factors such as interest rates or legislation
4 indirect influence on competitors through strategy; direct influence through technological innovation and legislative developments.

Challenging questions

13 Amelia is the owner of a business called Your Elegance. Your Elegance purchases second-hand evening gowns, alters them and resells them at a very reasonable price. The seamstresses working for Amelia have extensive accumulated experience in dealing with the delicate fabric of evening gowns. This is known as ...... **resource** which belongs in the ...... **environment**.

1 a tangible; market
2 an intangible; market
3 a tangible; micro-
4 an intangible; micro-.

14 Andile has started a small soccer shop in Polokwane to cater to the needs of the local players. With the 2010 Soccer World Cup approaching fast, which one of the following would represent a **threat** to his business?

1 A big Sportsman's Warehouse with a dedicated soccer section is opening in the main street in town early in 2010
2 Andile would like to expand his store but his loan application at ABSA bank has been turned down
3 With an influx of international tourists, Andile's sales should increase if he can manage to secure 'Proudly South African' soccer kits.
4 One of Andile's staff members, Paulina, just had a baby and will be on maternity leave for the rest of the year, leaving Andile to attend to the shop alone.

15 Match the **term** in Block A with the **correct characteristic** in Block B.

BLOCK A	
a	Micro-environment
b	Market environment
c	Macro-environment

BLOCK B	
(i)	The new Liquor Act will have a significant impact on Mandla's new shebeen
(ii)	TJ's Diner's mission statement is 'To serve hearty meals with heart'
(iii)	Sam has been unfairly dismissed and has approached the CCMA for help
(iv)	Lara has appointed a communication expert to enhance multi-racial communications
(v)	Kogiso is doing intensive research on the competitors for his new IT shop in Vryheid

1 a (iv)   b (i)   c (ii)
2 a (iv)   b (iii) c (v)
3 a (ii)   b (v)   c (i)
4 a (ii)   b (iii) c (v)

16 Which **one** of the following is a **social environmental trend** that companies need to be aware of?
   1 The GDP (Gross Domestic Product) of South Africa in the last quarter of 2008 was 3.1%
   2 Eskom proposes an increase of 45% per annum for the next three years to combat the cost of energy in South Africa
   3 The Gautrain will be the first rapid-rail service in South Africa available to commuters early in 2010
   4 South African population figures are: black 79.7%; white 9.1%; coloured 8.8%; Asian (Indian) 2.2%.

17 You are explaining **the competitive forces** to your friend by means of the diagram below.
   Which **threat** is left out in the diagram?
   1 substitutes
   2 competitors
   3 the market
   4 intermediaries.

18 Which of the following statements are **correct** concerning the business environment?
   a Management has complete control over the micro-environment
   b The market environment includes both suppliers and competitors
   c The market environment exerts no influence on the micro-environment
   d An enterprise's mission and goals are variables within the micro-environment.
   1 a, b
   2 a, b, c
   3 a, b, d
   4 c, d

Read the brief case study below and answer questions 19–20 that follow:

Strike looms at Sasol

A strike in the industrial chemical sectors may be unavoidable, trade union Solidarity warned on Thursday. Solidarity decided not to accept the sector's final wage offer of 11% plus an additional 1% increase in January 2009. The trade union, that contends that only an increase of 12% will be accepted, has already been issued a strike certificate allowing its members to go on strike within 48 hours of issuing notice.

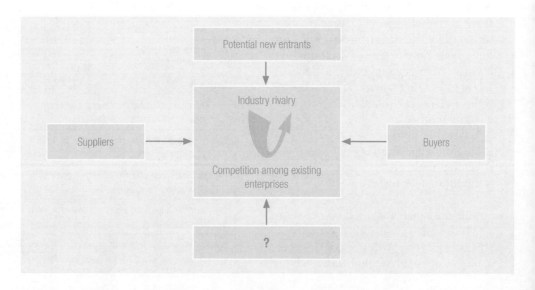

'Employees cannot survive on the current offer,' said Solidarity spokesperson for the chemical industry, Marius Croucamp. 'Inflation, the increase in municipal rates and the new property tax regulation place enormous pressure on employees' budgets and the only solution is a more favourable wage increase,' Croucamp said.

The trade union said that Sasol, the largest employer in this sector, was benefitting from record Brent crude oil prices as well as the weak rand/dollar exchange rate. 'It is expected that Sasol will make a profit of approximately R25 billion for the year 2007/08. This remarkable profit indicates that a wage increase of 12% definitely is within their financial capabilities,' pointed out Croucamp.

At the same time as Sasol is making unprecedented profits by producing oil from coal, the world has seen an increase in the production of cleaner and more sustainable energy in the form of 'biofuels'. Biofuels are created either through the production of ethanol from plant sources such as sugar cane and maize or the production of biodiesel from oil-producing plants sources such as soya beans and algae. And it has not taken long for South African companies to get onboard in terms of biofuel production. In fact the Koega Industrial Development Zone (IDZ) in the Eastern Cape is so serious about getting its biofuel plant off the ground that it has found an investor that is already hard at work building a R1.5 billion soya bean processing plant.

Source: Adapted from an article which appeared on Fin24. com. Article accessed at www.fin24.com/articles/default/ display_article.aspx?articleId=1518-24_235125. I-Net Bridge. 3 July 2008.

19 The **high inflation rate** mentioned by Mr Croucamp is a variable in Sasol's ...... which forms part of the ...... environment over which Sasol management has ...... control.
1 social; macro; indirect
2 economic; market; direct
3 social; market; no
4 economic; macro; no.

20 The high inflation rate and increased petrol prices have a direct impact on the purchasing power of consumers. A **consumer's purchasing** power is a variable in Sasol's ...... environment and is represented by the consumer's ...... income.
1 social; total
2 economic; total
3 market; disposable
4 economic; disposable.

SUGGESTED SOLUTIONS TO THE FIRST FIVE QUESTIONS

Q	A
1	2
2	3
3	4
4	3
5	1

Corporate social responsibility

Corporate social responsibility has become an important part of any business. Businesses operate in and have an impact on a wider social environment. Corporate social responsibility means that organisations take responsibility for the impact of their activities on customers, suppliers, employees, shareholders, communities and other stakeholders, as well as the environment.

MULTIPLE-CHOICE QUESTIONS

Easy questions

1 Corporate citizenship ...
   1 measures the financial, social and environmental impacts of business
   2 refers to how a company's objectives, strategies and decision-making structures are developed, implemented and monitored and also relates to the extent to which the company is accountable to its shareholders and stakeholders
   3 is the extent to which an organisation gains acceptance in a foreign market
   4 is about proactive efforts by companies to make a positive contribution to society.

2 The ... is at the heart of good corporate citizenship and guides stakeholders to determine what they want from the company and what they consider to be the issues and culture of the company.
   1 triple bottom line
   2 stakeholder engagement
   3 global reporting initiative
   4 King 3 Report.

3 The term .... refers to the increasing expectations for companies to publicly report not only on financial matters but also on social and environmental issues.
   1 sustainable development
   2 sustainable reporting
   3 corporate governance
   4 triple bottom line.

4 In an effort to show your parents what you have learnt in the business management module, you tell them that, 'The **primary stakeholders** of the company are ...'
   a the environmental NGOs
   b the executive board members
   c the government
   d the media
   e the shareholders.
   Circle the most appropriate combination:
   1 a, b, d
   2 a, c, d
   3 b, c, e
   4 a, b, c, d

5 In an effort to show your parents what you have learnt in the business management module, you tell them that, 'The **secondary stakeholders** of the company are ...'
   a the environmental NGOs
   b the executive board members.
   c the government
   d the media
   e the shareholders.

Select the most appropriate combination
1 a, d
2 a, b, c
3 a, b, d
4 a, c, d
5 a, b, c, d

Moderate questions

6 While a company's bottom line tra-
ditionally refers to its financial profit
or loss, the .... refers to the need to
consider the social and environmental
impacts as well.
1 balanced scorecard
2 triple bottom line
3 social investment index
4 corporate social investment index
   (CSI).

7 Recognising and responding to emerging niche markets allows companies to
translate good corporate citizenship into
...
1 corporate social opportunity
2 total quality management
3 corporate social investment
4 sustainability reporting.

8 Which **one** of the following statements
about corporate citizenship is **incorrect**?
1 Corporate citizenship suggests that
   companies will benefit if they contribute to the welfare of people in the
   community
2 All aspects of corporate citizenship have an economic benefit for
   companies
3 The business case for corporate
   citizenship refers to the argument
   that being a good corporate citi-
   zen can contribute to a company's
   profitability
4 Good corporate citizenship practices
   can create market opportunities and
   increase competitiveness of companies that use innovation to develop
   products or services based on sustainability criteria.

9 Which **one** of the following statements
about the stakeholder engagement process is **incorrect**?
1 It is a process that allows stakeholders to determine what they want
   from the company and what they
   consider to be the issues and culture
   of the company
2 It involves mapping the internal and
   the external stakeholders and defines
   their roles in and impact on the
   company
3 It is interchangeable with the company's public relations function
4 The company may use instruments
   such as questionnaires, market
   research, and personal visits to gather information on its stakeholders
5 It is a process that can be seen to
   be at the heart of good corporate
   citizenship.

10 Indicate which of the following statements about corporate citizenship are
correct?
a The triple bottom line refers to the
   need to consider the social, environmental and socio-cultural impacts in
   an organisation
b Stakeholder engagement is at the
   heart of good corporate citizenship
c The business case for corporate
   citizenship refers to the argument
   that being a good corporate citi-
   zen can contribute to a company's
   profitability
d Practising corporate citizenship
   guarantees economic benefits for a
   company.
   1 a, b
   2 a, c
   3 b, c
   4 b, d

11 Themba explains to his son that there
are various local imperatives for organisations that can promote the implementation of corporate citizenship.

One such imperative is a progressive document which explicitly defines and substantiates concepts such as corporate citizenship, social responsibility and triple bottom line. This document is known as the ....
1　Kyoto Protocol
2　JSE SRI index
3　King 3 Report
4　Dow Jones sustainability index.

12　There are various initiatives and imperatives in South Africa that drive corporate citizenship. One such initiative, known as the ...... is very important as it explicitly defines and substantiates concepts such as 'corporate citizenship', 'social responsibility', 'stakeholder engagement' and 'sustainability reporting'.
1　JSE SRI index
2　Global Reporting initiative (GRI)
3　King 2 Report
4　AA 1000 Framework.

Challenging questions

13　In an attempt to assist the victims of the 2008 xenophobic attacks in South Africa, the university held a charity golf day to raise funds for foreign students who lost their study material or books in the xenophobic attacks. These actions are indicative of the university fulfilling its ...... imperative.
1　triple bottom line
2　sustainable development
3　corporate social responsibility
4　total quality management.

14　Match the term in Block A with the description in Block B.

BLOCK A
Term
a　Sustainable development
b　Corporate social investment
c　Sustainability reporting
d　Corporate governance

BLOCK B
Description
(i)　Refers to the increasing expectations for companies to publicly report not just on financial matters, but also on social and environmental issues
(ii)　Refers to how a company's objectives, strategy and decision-making structures are developed, implemented and monitored
(iii)　Refers to the need to improve the lives of poor people and to protect the natural environment
(iv)　Refers to a company's philanthropic initiatives, such as sponsorships for students

1　a (iii)　b (iv)　c (i)　d (ii)
2　a (iv)　b (iii)　c (ii)　d (i)
3　a (i)　b (iii)　c (ii)　d (iv)
4　a (ii)　b (i)　c (iv)　d (iii)

15　All businesses have stakeholders who are affected by or who can have an affect on the business. Which of the following can be classified as **external stakeholders** of a business?
a　executive board members
b　shareholders
c　customers
d　a group of employees represented by a shop steward
e　NGOs.
　　1　a, c
　　2　a, b, d
　　3　b, c, e

4 a, b, c, d
5 a, b, c, d, e

16 Which of the following statements about the stakeholder engagement process are **correct**?
   a It is a process that allows stakeholders to determine what they want from the company and what they consider to be the issues and culture of the company
   b It involves mapping the internal and the external stakeholders and defines their roles in and impact on the company
   c It is interchangeable with the company's public relations function
   d The company may use instruments such as questionnaires, market research, and personal visits to gather information on its stakeholders
   e It is a process that can be seen to be at the heart of good corporate citizenship.
      1 a, b
      2 a, b, c, e
      3 a, b, d, c
      4 b, c, d
      5 a, b, d, e

Read the case study below and answer questions 17 and 18 that follow:

Mark is the CEO of a big corporation, Dark Gems that mines diamonds in West Africa. Dark Gems has been very successful, and has recently been listed on the JSE. However, it has received various complaints stating that it is not adhering to the principles of corporate citizenship, and this has started to affect the corporation's business.

17 Recently, the corporation asked Mark to develop a policy on corporate citizenship that is based on the principle of the triple bottom line. Which **one** of the following is **correct**?
   1 Dark Gems will in future contribute 3% of its profit to building schools in the surrounding areas to educate the children of the local workforce and launch a programme that will teach the local women about sustainable farming practices
   2 Dark Gems will have a section of its mine closed and rehabilitated as a conservation area for a threatened species of bird that is found only in that area
   3 Dark Gems has sponsored a local soccer team. This has allowed the team to compete in a prestigious tournament in South Africa
   4 Dark Gems will in future operate its mines in such a way that it contributes to the social wellbeing of its employees, protects the environment from harmful practices and continues to grow its profits.

18 While compiling his report on corporate citizenship, Mark identified certain stakeholders. Which of the following are **stakeholders** in Dark Gems?
   a Mark, the CEO
   b the local community living around the mine
   c Isanda Diamonds, who purchases the diamonds for jewellery
   d the international media, who are reporting on the mine's environmental policy.
      1 a, b, d
      2 b, c, d
      3 a, b, c, d
      4 None of the above

19 Themba is the CEO of a big company. Themba's son has just graduated from business school and will start working for his dad's company soon and will, one day, take over the company. Themba explains to his son that corporate citizenship is nowadays a very important concept in business. He explains to his son that good corporate citizenship practices will, at the end of the day, have

positive implications for the financial bottom line and that the benefits to the business can come in a variety of forms. Which of the following are examples of benefits received by Themba's company as a result of good corporate citizenship practices?

a Themba's company uses energy-saving technology that saves the company money on its monthly electricity bill

b Themba's company sends his employees on team building activities throughout the year. This has aided his employees to work well in teams

c Themba's company uses recycled materials and solar panel technology to generate energy, this has saved the company a lot of money

d Themba ensures that there is continuous training and education available to the employees in the business. This keeps the employees motivated and productivity levels high.

1 a, c
2 a, d
3 b, d
4 b, c
5 None of the above.

20 Match the term in Block A with the correct definition in Block B.

BLOCK A	
a	Sustainability reporting
b	Triple bottom line
c	Corporate social responsibility
d	Sustainability development

BLOCK B	
(i)	The need to improve the lives of poor people and to protect the natural environment
(ii)	The increasing expectations for companies to publicly report on not only financial reporting but also on social and environmental issues
(iii)	The need to consider the social and environmental impacts as well as the financial profit and loss
(iv)	Synonymous with corporate citizenship
(v)	Refers to how a company's objectives, strategy and decision making structures are developed, implemented and monitored

1 a (ii)   b (i)   c (iv)   d (iii)
2 a (ii)   b (iii)   c (iv)   d (i)
3 a (iii)   b (iv)   c (i)   d (ii)
4 a (iv)   b (iii)   c (ii)   d (i)

SUGGESTED SOLUTIONS TO THE FIRST FIVE QUESTIONS

Q	A
1	4
2	2
3	2
4	3
5	1

Planning

Planning is the first fundamental activity of the management process. Planning is like a road-map, giving an organisation the directions it must follow to accomplish the determined goals. In other words, planning involves determining the mission and goals of an organisation, the ways in which the organisation will achieve these goals, and the deployment of the necessary resources to realise them.

MULTIPLE-CHOICE QUESTIONS

Easy questions

1 Management will constantly bear which of the following facets in mind when developing alternative plans during the planning process?
   a external factors
   b strong and weak points
   c rational decision making
   d strategic planning.
   1 a, b
   2 b, d
   3 a, b, c
   4 b, c, d
   5 a, b, c, d

2 Mr Dlamini is a newly appointed manager for General Motors, Hatfield. Rank the basic management tasks that he will have to perform in the correct order.
   a planning
   b organising
   c leading
   d control.
   1 a, b, c, d
   2 b, c, d, a
   3 c, a, b, d
   4 d, a, b, c

3 Identify which of the following statements indicate the **importance** of planning.
   a Planning promotes cooperation
   b Planning gives direction
   c Planning is more important in smaller businesses
   d Planning guarantees profit.
   1 a, b
   2 a, d
   3 a, c, d
   4 b, c, d
   5 a, b, c, d

4 The sequential steps in the **planning process** are:
   1 developing plans, goal-setting, feedback
   2 goal-setting, mission statement, implementation
   3 mission statement, developing plans, feedback
   4 goal-setting, developing plans, implementation.

5 Which of the following are requirements for setting **sound objectives**?
   a Objectives have to be measurable
   b Objectives should be set consistently
   c Goal setting should be integrated into the remuneration system of an organisation
   d Management must ensure that employees accept the objectives.

1 a, b, c
2 a, b, d
3 a, c, d
4 b, c, d
5 a, b, c, d

Moderate questions

6 Which of the following are characteristics of **strategic planning**? Mark the correct answer.
   a It has a time-frame of three to 10 years
   b It is focused on an organisation as a whole
   c It is future oriented
   d It does concern itself with details.
      1 a, b
      2 a, c, d
      3 b, c, d
      4 a, b, c
      5 a, b, c, d

7 Which of the following statements are **wrong**?
   Management must realise the importance of goals because ...
   a goals provide guidance and direction in an organisation
   b goals provide an effective means of evaluation and control
   c goals represent a burden to employees
   d realistic goals facilitate planning
   e goals lead inevitably to success.
      1 a, c
      2 b, d
      3 c, e
      4 a, b, d
      5 c, d, e

8 Which **one** of the following **long-term strategies** entails the takeover of firms that supply a business with raw materials?
      1 vertical integration
      2 product development
      3 horizontal integration
      4 market development.

9 Match the **management level** in Block A with the corresponding **organisational objective** in Block B.

BLOCK A
Management level
a Top management
b Middle management
c Lower management

BLOCK B
Organisational objective
(i)   The mission of the organisation
(ii)   Functional objectives
(iii) Operational objectives

1 a (i)   b (ii)   c (iii)
2 a (i)   b (iii)   c (ii)
3 a (ii)   b (i)   c (iii)
4 a (iii) b (i)   c (ii)

10 An enterprise taking over a competitor in order to eliminate the competition, is an example of ...
   1 diversification
   2 horizontal integration
   3 innovation
   4 vertical integration.

11 If a supermarket chain such as Pick n Pay was to purchase a bakery such as Sasko Bread with the intention of baking its own bread and selling it in its Pick n Pay stores, this would be an example of ...
   1 market development
   2 horizontal integration
   3 innovation
   4 vertical integration.

12 Shoprite Checkers, the supermarket chain, has set itself the objective of increasing market share from 20% to 80% within the next five years. The **goal**

set by Shoprite Checkers is an example of a ... which is formulated by ... management.

1 functional goal, middle
2 functional goal, top
3 long-term goal, middle
4 long–term goal, top.

Challenging questions

Read the case study below and answer questions 13 and 14:

Nutri-Grain, Kellogg's – identifying the problem

The Kellogg's Company is the world's leading producer of breakfast cereals and convenience foods, with household brands such as Rice Krispies, Special K and Nutri-Grain. When Nutri-Grain was first launched in 1997, it was immediately successful, gaining almost 50% share of the growing cereal bar market in just two years. It maintained growth sales until 2002 through expanding the original product with new developments in flavour and format.

However by mid-2004, Nutri-Grain found its sales declining whilst the market continued to grow at a rate of 15%. Competitor brands from both Kellogg's itself (e.g. All-Bran bars) and other manufacturers (e.g. Alpen bars) offered the same benefits and this slowed down sales and chipped away at Nutri-Grain's market position. Kellogg's had to decide whether the problem with Nutri-Grain was the market or the product, or both. The market had grown by over 15% and competitors' market share had increased whilst Nutri-Grain sales in 2003 had declined. Kellogg's decided to try and extend the life of the product rather than withdraw it from the market which meant developing an extension strategy.

Having recognised the problems, Kellogg's then developed solutions to re-brand and re-launch the product in 2005. They decided in order to re-launch the product; they needed to renew the brand image. Kellogg's looked at the core features that made the brand different and modelled the new brand image on these. New packaging was introduced to unify the

brand image and an improved pricing structure for the stores and supermarkets was developed. The Nutri-Grain brand achieved a retail sales growth rate of almost three times that of the market and, most importantly, growth was maintained after the initial re-launch. Nutri-Grain remains a growing brand and product within the Kellogg's product family.

Source: www.thetimes100.co.uk.

13 Which **long-term strategy** did Kellogg's adopt in an attempt to extend the life of the product?
1 diversification
2 product development
3 market development
4 innovation.

14 If Kellogg's decided to withdraw the product from the market instead of extending the life of the product, the company would be adopting a **strategy** known as ...
1 diversification
2 liquidation
3 divestiture
4 rationalisation.

15 In expanding its share of the retail and grocery market in South Africa, the Shoprite group has embarked on a major campaign to acquire grocery retailers similar to it. This has led to a marked increase in market share for the group.
What kind of **long-term strategy** has been adopted by Shoprite?
1 market development
2 concentration growth
3 horizontal integration
4 diversification.

16 Kulula.com has taken the decision to expand its product offering to include low-cost vehicle hire. The company plans to roll out this new product offering within the next five years.

This is an example of a/an ...... goal.
1 operational
2 strategic
3 functional
4 tactical.

17 In response to Kulula.com's new product offering, the marketing manager at SAA, Phindiwe, plans to increase her expenditure on advertising by 20% over the next three years. What she does not know however is that the Chief Financial Officer at SAA is planning to cut the marketing department's budget in the short term.

Phindiwe's goal does not meet the requirements of a good goal as it lacks ...
1 measurability
2 acceptability
3 horizontal consistency
4 vertical consistency.

18 Which of the following are examples of **strategic decisions**?
a Woolworths' decision to concentrate its business not only on clothing, but also to move into the grocery market
b Standard Bank's decision to open a new branch in Hermanus
c Unisa's decision to send more audio cassettes to students
d Kodak's decision to return to South Africa
e Nissan's decision to enter the small passenger car market with the introduction of the Nissan Micra.
    1 a, b, c
    2 a, b, d
    3 a, d, e
    4 b, c, e
    5 a, b, c, d, e

19 Over the past few years South African Breweries (SABMiller) has embarked on a very clear strategy of acquiring other similar breweries including Millers in the United States and Pilsner Urquel in the Czech Republic.

The **long-term strategy** adopted by SABMiller is known as ...
1 concentration growth
2 market development
3 horizontal integration
4 vertical integration.

20 One of the main ingredients in the brewing of the beer produced by SABMiller is hops. If SABMiller decided to take over its suppliers of hops to ensure a better quality of supply, this **long-term strategy** would be known as ...
1 product development
2 innovation
3 vertical integration
4 horizontal integration.

SUGGESTED SOLUTIONS TO THE FIRST FIVE QUESTIONS

Q	A
1	1
2	1
3	1
4	4
5	5

Organising

Organising is the second fundamental task of management and involves the development of a structure or framework. Within this structure, the tasks that need to be performed in order to accomplish goals and the resources necessary to perform these tasks are allocated to particular individuals and departments. Organising enables the employees concerned to work effectively towards the organisation's mission and goals as set out during the first fundamental management task of planning.

MULTIPLE-CHOICE QUESTIONS

Easy questions

1 **Line** authority means ...
   1 the authority of a manager in a department other than his own
   2 authority delegated through the line of command
   3 authority which subordinates accept from the bottom
   4 indirect authority.

2 **Staff** authority means ...
   1 the authority of a manager in a department other than his own
   2 authority which subordinates accept from the bottom
   3 authority delegated through the line of command
   4 direct authority
   5 indirect authority.

3 A **broad** organisational structure will probably lead to ...
   a underutilised managers
   b a greater span of management
   c many subordinates for each manager
   d less intensive supervision of subordinates.
   1 a, b, c
   2 a, b, d
   3 b, c, d

   4 a, c, d
   5 a, b, c, d

4 A **tall or narrow** organisation structure will probably lead to ...
   1 managers being over worked
   2 a greater span of management
   3 less subordinates for each manager
   4 less intensive supervision of subordinates.

5 Which of the following are basic forms of **departmentalisation**?
   a according to product
   b according to location
   c according to resources
   d according to customers.
   1 a, b
   2 a, b, c
   3 a, b, d
   4 a, b, c, d

Moderate questions

6 **Specialisation** became part of the organising process because ...
   1 labour productivity started declining
   2 the use of assembly lines increased
   3 the specialised skills of individuals increased
   4 of constant pressure to split up the total task into smaller units.

7   Which of the following reasons justifies **specialisation** in an organisation?
   a individuals perform a task with expert skills
   b eliminating non-productive transfer time
   c increased productivity due to specialised equipment
   d decreased labour cost
   e determination of an employee's role within an organisation.
      1 a, b
      2 a, b, c
      3 a, b, c, d
      4 a, b, c, d, e

8   Which **one** of the following statements about **specialisation** is **incorrect**?
   1 The main purpose of specialisation is to increase productivity
   2 Excessive specialisation may have a negative effect on productivity
   3 Workers who perform highly specialised jobs may become bored and demotivated
   4 Specialisation can only be applied at operational levels.

9   A manager's **span of management** is determined by ...
   1 the number of subordinates who report directly to him
   2 the number of subordinates at lower levels
   3 the number of subordinates on the same level
   4 the size of the enterprise.

10 A key principle of organising is the concept of **span of management**.
      A narrow span of management leads to ...
   a a tall organisational structure
   b a long chain of command
   c overworked managers
   d slow decision making
   e a flat organisational structure.
      1 a, b, c
      2 a, b, d
      3 a, c, d
      4 b, c, d
      5 c, d, e

11 Which of the following factors will influence how an organization is structured?
   a the stability of the business environment
   b the strategy of the business
   c the size of the business
   d the location of the business
   e the organisational culture.
      1 a, b, d, e
      2 a, b, c, e
      3 b, c, d, e
      4 a, b, c, d

12 Sarah decides to open a sandwich delivery business from her house. She makes the sandwiches herself, delivering her sandwiches door to door within her community. Soon, her sandwiches become so popular that she decides to employ more people to help her with the work load. Sarah realises that in order to increase productivity, she will need to separate the different tasks into smaller units. Sarah hires a chef to make the sandwiches and three people to do the deliveries so that she can focus on the marketing and management aspects of the business. The division of labour and the way that Sarah separated the tasks into smaller units to improve productivity is known as:
   1 job design
   2 specialisation
   3 departmentalisation
   4 job enlargement.

Challenging questions

13 Thabo is the manager of an advertising company. The business is divided into various business units including sales, marketing, media, customer insight,

and products and services. Thabo's advertising is therefore **departmentalised** according to:
1 function
2 product
3 location
4 customer.

14 The authority delegated down the chain of command from the CEO to the General Manager of Operations is known as ... **authority**. If, however, the Manager of Computers and Software were to give instructions to the General Manager of Marketing, in the form of advice or recommendations based on his or her specialist knowledge, this would be referred to as ... **authority**.
1 functional, line
2 staff, line
3 line, functional
4 line, staff.

15 To overcome some of the inherent problems with conventional organisational structures, managers have started to structure their organisations in new and different ways. One of the contemporary approaches that has emerged allows for both horizontal and vertical lines of authority to occur in the same structure.

This approach to structuring organisations is particularly suited to large organisations and to those handling many projects. It is known as the ... structure.
1 virtual
2 boundaryless
3 team
4 matrix.

16 Match the form of **departmentalisation** in Block A with the appropriate example in Block B.

BLOCK A	
a	According to function
b	According to location
c	According to customer
d	According to product

BLOCK B	
(i)	The company has departments which focus on selling equipment to the motor industry, the computer industry and the Navy
(ii)	The company has departments that specialise in selling its products in Gauteng and KwaZulu-Natal respectively
(iii)	Sasol has various business units which focus on the production of different products such as Sasol Synthetic Fuels, Sasol Fertilizers, and Sasol Plastics
(iv)	The company has grouped all its financial activities under the financial manager or section and all its marketing activities under the marketing manager or section

1 a (iv)   b (ii)   c (i)   d (iii)
2 a (ii)   b (iv)   c (iii)   d (i)
3 a (iii)   b (iv)   c (i)   d (ii)
4 a (ii)   b (iii)   c (iv)   d (i)

Read the following brief case study and answer question 17 and 18 that follow:

Innovative Ink Ltd. design cards (birthday cards, greeting cards, Christmas cards) in a step-by-step process – artists and writers rarely spoke to one another and the employees who created the lettering worked in another building.

Due to delays and rework, it sometimes took the company more than two years to create and produce a new greeting card. Now Innovative Ink Ltd. puts teams of employees from every department in the same room and empowers each team to take charge of specific cards. Artists, lithographers, writers, designers and photographers share ideas, critique their own work and make their own decisions without waiting for management permission. Although the decision making is decentralised in terms of the team approach being used, management thought it wise to appoint team leaders on a three month rotational basis. The cycle time for getting new cards to the market has been cut in half. For employees the change has brought more responsibility and greater job satisfaction. The change in structure and organising has also brought about new ideas and thinking in the company. Innovative Ink Ltd. recently also introduced its new line of postcards which are doing extremely well in the market.

17 How was Innovative Ink Ltd. **departmentalised** before the company set about changing the way the business is organised?
1 according to customer
2 according to function
3 according to location
4 according to product.

18 How is Innovative Ink Ltd. **departmentalised** now?
1 according to customer
2 according to function
3 according to location
4 according to product.

19 Match the **type of authority** in Block A with the correct description in Block B.

BLOCK A	
a	Functional authority
b	Line authority
c	Staff authority

BLOCK B	
(i)	Sarah, the front office manager at a Protea Hotel instructs the receptionists to inform guests about the special weekend rate
(ii)	Sello, a university lecturer, approaches the university's Market Research Bureau for advice and assistance regarding a research project he is busy with
(iii)	Thabo is the human resource manager at a factory and instructs the production manager to abide by certain human resource policies in the factory

1 a (ii)   b (i)   c (iii)
2 a (i)   b (iii)   c (ii)
3 a (iii)   b (i)   c (ii)
4 a (iii)   b (ii)   c (i)

20 Match the **term** in Block A with the correct description in Block B.

BLOCK A	
a	Responsibility
b	Line authority
c	Staff authority
d	Span of management

BLOCK B	
(i)	The manager has twenty employees who report directly to him/her.
(ii)	The employee must be able to account for the work they have done.
(iii)	The marketing research department makes recommendations to the marketing manager, based on research results.
(iv)	The managing director instructs the marketing manager on goals to be achieved, while the marketing manager tells the advertising manager what to do to achieve these goals.

1 a (i)   b (ii)   c (iii)   d (iv)
2 a (ii)   b (iv)   c (iii)   d (i)
3 a (iii)   b (iv)   c (i)   d (ii)
4 a (ii)   b (iii)   c (iv)   d (i)

SUGGESTED SOLUTIONS TO THE FIRST FIVE QUESTIONS

Q	A
1	2
2	5
3	3
4	3
5	3

Leading

In order to be successful, organisations need managers who are also good leaders. Managers use the leading function to effectively manage the human resources in their organisations. They use authority and power to influence and motivate their employees to willingly strive to achieve organisational goals. Leadership theories and models as well as contemporary issues in leadership help managers understand what leadership entails. Effective leadership depends on constant communication, a crucial element of the leading function, with individual employees, groups and teams within an organisation.

MULTIPLE-CHOICE QUESTIONS

Easy questions

1 Which of the following statements on aspects of **leadership** are **correct**?
  a Authority gives a leader the right to give commands to subordinates
  b Authority denotes the right of a leader to demand actions from subordinates
  c Authority denotes the ability of a leader to influence the behaviour of others without necessarily using his or her authority
  d Responsibility is a manager's ability to influence his or her employees' behaviour.
    1 a, b
    2 a, b, d
    3 a, c, d
    4 b, c, d
    5 a, b, c, d

2 Which of the following are components of management's **leadership task**?
  a leadership
  b motivation
  c productivity
  d knowledge of individual behaviour
  e communication.
    1 a, b, e
    2 a, b, d, e

    3 a, c, d, e
    4 b, c, d, e
    5 a, b, c, d, e

3 **Employee performance** in organisations is determined mainly by three factors:
    1 motivation, ability and resources
    2 desire, willingness and resources to do the job
    3 salary, motivation and work environment
    4 capability, willingness and resources to do the job.

4 **Social loafing** refers to ...
    1 the tendency of individuals to put in less effort when working in a group
    2 a particular campaign that employees might embark on
    3 the way that a group will stand together as a unit
    4 employees from the same department who meet regularly to discuss ways of improving the quality of the work environment
    5 a small number of employees working together on a project.

5 A **manager** is likely to be a **successful leader** if he/she ...
    1 uses his/her formal authority to motivate his/her subordinates

2 can activate his/her subordinates to carry out his/her instructions

3 can influence his/her subordinates positively without using authority

4 uses legitimate power to get his/her subordinates to carry out their duties.

Moderate questions

6 When an employee is appointed to a certain managerial post, he/she will have been given ... power.
1 referent
2 personal
3 coercive
4 expert
5 legitimate.

7 A manager has ... power if his/her subordinates obey him/her simply because they like, respect and identify with him/her.
1 expert
2 legitimate
3 coercive
4 formal
5 referent.

8 Subordinates in organisations do not only work as individuals but often in groups. The types of groups in an organisation can differ. ... groups, such as committees are established by management to carry out specific duties.
1 Task
2 Functional
3 Interest
4 Cross-functional.

9 Managers cannot be effective leaders if their employees do not perceive them as being trustworthy. Which of the following form part of the **five dimensions of trust**?
a integrity
b competence
c friendliness
d loyalty
e openness.

1 a, b
2 a, b, c
3 a, b, c, d
4 a, b, d, e
5 a, b, c, d, e

10 Blake and Mouton developed the '**Managerial Grid**' – an instrument that identifies various leadership styles based on a two-dimensional grid. In developing the grid they measured two dimensions, namely, ... and ... .
1 concern for people; concern for profit
2 concern for personality; concern for profit
3 concern for people; concern for production
4 concern for personality; concern for production.

11 Every group in an organisation is different in terms of its structure or set of characteristics. Which statements about the **characteristics** of a **group** are correct?
a group size affects the group's overall performance
b group composition does not influence a group's performance
c status in groups can only be formal
d norms are standards shared by members of a group and develop from the interaction between members.
1 a, b
2 a, c
3 b, c
4 a, d

12 Which of the following statements on **groups** are **correct**?
a The success of a group depends on the quality of its leadership
b The success of a leader depends on the members' acceptance of his or her leadership
c Group pressure influences most members to adhere to group norms
d All groups have a strong sense of

solidarity amongst their members.

1 b, c
2 c, d
3 a, b, c
4 a, b, d
5 a, b, c, d

Challenging questions

13 **University of Iowa** researchers identified **three basic leadership styles**. Which one of the following is not a leadership style identified by the University of Iowa studies?

1 autocratic leadership
2 democratic leadership
3 participative leadership
4 laissez-faire leadership.

14 When an employee is appointed to a certain managerial post, he/she will have been given ... power. This is a form of ... power.

1 expert; personal
2 legitimate; positional
3 coercive; positional
4 referent; personal.

15 A manager has ... power if her subordinates obey her simply because they like, respect and identify with her. This is a form of ... power.

1 expert; personal
2 legitimate; positional
3 coercive; positional
4 referent; personal.

16 Peter Mashiba is the CEO of a furniture company. As the CEO he has the right to discipline or dismiss employees who are not performing well. Peter, therefore, possesses ... power which is a form of ... power.

1 legitimate; positional
2 legitimate; personal
3 expert; positional
4 expert; personal.

17 The managing director of a local computer business must inform his employees that the business will soon merge with a large international business. Which of the following are prerequisites for **effective communication** between the managing director and his employees?

a The communication channel must suit the employees
b The message must be interpreted correctly by the employees
c The managing director must determine whether the message has been correctly interpreted
d The employees must be able to grasp the concept the managing director wishes to convey.

1 a, b
2 c, d
3 a, b, c
4 a, b, c, d

18 Match the leadership component in Block A with the correct description in Block B.

BLOCK A	
a	Authority
b	Power
c	Responsibility
d	Delegation

BLOCK B	
(i)	The influence that leaders exert over their subordinates
(ii)	As CEO of a computer company, Mr Smith has an obligation to achieve organisational goals by ensuring the required activities are performed
(iii)	Process of assigning responsibility and authority for achieving organisational goals
(iv)	As manager of a restaurant, Mr Ndluvo has the right to give instructions, allocate resources and demand action from his subordinates

1 a (ii)   b (iii)   c (iv)   d (i)
2 a (iii)   b (ii)   c (i)   d (iv)
3 a (iv)   b (i)   c (ii)   d (iii)
4 a (iii)   b (ii)   c (iv)   d (i)

19 Match the **type of power** in Block A with the examples of people who possess that type of power in Block B.

BLOCK A	
a	Legitimate power
b	Referent power
c	Coercive power
d	Expert power

BLOCK B	
(i)	A group of gangsters
(ii)	Bill Gates
(iii)	Nelson Mandela
(iv)	The CEO of a company

1 a (i)   b (ii)   c (iii) d (iv)
2 a (i)   b (iii)   c (iv)   d (ii)
3 a (iv)   b (ii)   c (i)   d (iii)
4 a (iv)   b (iii)   c (i)   d (ii)

20 When leading a business, it often is necessary to create **teams** to achieve certain objectives. Match the type of team in Block A with the correct description in Block B.

BLOCK A	
a	Problem-solving teams
b	Self-managed teams
c	Cross-functional teams

BLOCK B	
(i)	Consists of two or more people who interact primarily to share information and make decisions that will help each member perform within his or her own area of responsibility
(ii)	Members take on responsibilities from their former managers and address problems in the work process

(iii)	Consists of employees from the same department who meet to discuss ways of improving quality, efficiency and the work environment
(iv)	Employees that share a common interest which satisfies the social needs of the members
(v)	Consists of employees at the same hierarchical level, but from different work areas who come together to accomplish a task

1 a (iii)   b (v)   c (ii)
2 a (iii)   b (ii)   c (v)
3 a (i)   b (ii)   c (iv)
4 a (iv)   b (v)   c (ii)

SUGGESTED SOLUTIONS TO THE FIRST FIVE QUESTIONS

Q	A
1	1
2	1
3	1
4	1
5	3

Controlling the management process

Control is the last of the four fundamental tasks of management. It is the final step of the management process, where the assessment of actual performance against planned performance initiates a new cycle of planning, organising, leading and control. The areas of control include physical resources, quality control, financial control, budgetary control, the control of information and of human resources.

MULTIPLE-CHOICE QUESTIONS

Easy questions

1 The **primary purpose** of the control process is to ...
1 establish the standards that have to be maintained
2 see that the results come as close as possible to the objectives
3 take corrective action to counteract deviations
4 continually analyse the cause of deviations.

2 Which of the following resources are **focal points** of control?
a physical resources
b financial resources
c information resources
d human resources.
1 a, b
2 a, b, d
3 c, d
4 b, c, d
5 a, b, c, d

3 The **characteristics** of an **effective control system** are ...
1 complexity and flexibility
2 integration and flexibility
3 creativity and integration
4 creativity and complexity.

4 Identify the **first step** in the **control process**?
1 establish standards
2 observe actual performance
3 evaluate deviations
4 take corrective action.

5 Identify the **last step** in the **control process**?
1 observe actual performance
2 establish standards
3 take corrective action
4 evaluate deviations.

Moderate questions

6 Which of the following statements concerning the **control process** are **correct**?
a as the size of a business increases it becomes easier to identify areas of weak performance
b an effective control system allows management to identify problems before they become critical for the organisation
c increasing competition results in ineffective cost and quality control
d control usually results in better quality.
1 a, b
2 b, c
3 a, c
4 b, d

7   Which of the following statements con-
    cerning **control** are **correct**?
    a Control means applying strict disci-
       pline to subordinates
    b Control means getting planning and
       performance to coincide
    c Control is the last fundamental task
       of the management process
    d Control is a continuous process.
       1 a, b
       2 b, d
       3 b, c, d
       4 a, c, d
       5 a, b, c, d

8   The **design** of a **control system** depends
    on which of the following **factors**?
    a nature of the business
    b complexity of the business
    c activities of the business
    d size of the business
    e structure of the business.
       1 a, b, c
       2 a, b, e
       3 b, c, d
       4 a, b, c, d, e
       5 a, c, d, e

9   Which of the following are **characteris-
    tics** of an **effective control system**?
    a The control system must be able to
       adjust to change
    b The control system must be a JIT
       system
    c The control system must be integrat-
       ed with planning
    c The control system must not hide
       mistakes and it should be objective.
       1 a, b, c
       2 b, c
       3 a, d
       4 a, c, d

10 Which of the following factors are
    characteristics of an **effective control
    system**?
    a timeliness
    b complexity

c integration with planning
d accuracy
e rigidity.
   1 a, b
   2 a, b, c
   3 a, c, d
   4 a, c, d, e
   5 a, b, c, d, e

11 Which of the following factors make
    control in the present day enterprise
    important?
    a rapid change in the business
       environment
    b increasing size of the organisation
    c the delegation of tasks to subordinates
    d the possibility of managers and sub-
       ordinates making poor decisions and
       committing errors
    e organising subordinates.
       1 a, b, c, d
       2 b, d
       3 a, c, d, e
       4 c, d

12 Control, as a management function,
    focuses on several areas. Which one
    of the following is not considered to be
    such an area?
    1 physical resources such as inventory
       and equipment
    2 financial resources such as debtor
       accounts and budgets
    3 promotional resources such as spon-
       sorships and special packaging
    4 information resources such as envi-
       ronmental scanning and economic
       forecasts.

Challenging questions

13 Managers in the organisation must
    exercise control over four key areas,
    namely physical, financial, information
    and human resources.
        Which of the following are control
    systems used during the control of
    inventory as a **physical resource**?

a total quality management (TQM)
b economic ordering quantity (EOQ)
c just-in-time (JIT)
d an operational budget
e equipment control.
1 a, c
2 b, c
3 b, c, d
4 a, c, d, e
5 a, b, c, e

14 Managers in the organisation must exercise control over four key areas, namely physical, financial, information and human resources.

Which of the following are control systems used in the **control of human resources**?
a equity analysis
b performance measurement
c affirmative action
d labour turnover
e absenteeism ratios.
1 a, c
2 b, c
3 b, d, e
4 a, c, d, e
5 a, b, c, e

15 Managers in the organisation must exercise control over four key areas, namely physical, financial, information and human resources. Which of the following are control systems used in the **control of financial resources**?
a ratio analysis
b benchmarking
c budgets
d variation measurement
e specification limits.
1 a, c
2 b, c
3 b, c, d
4 a, c, d, e
5 a, b, c, e

16 The **main** instrument used to control an organisation's **human resources** is ...
1 labour turnover analysis
2 performance measurement
3 absenteeism analysis
4 compensation management.

17 Sophie has a manufacturing company. She wants to keep inventory costs as low as possible provided the method she uses does not cause shortages or delay the manufacturing process. Which of the following **control systems** can she use in order to **control her inventory**?
a EOQ (economic ordering quantity)
b ratio analysis
c performance measurement
d just-in-time (JIT).
1 a, b
2 c, d
3 a, d
4 b, c

Study the diagram below and then answer questions 18 and 19 which follow.

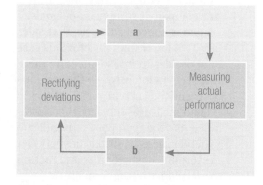

The diagram above refers to the **control process**.

18 In the diagram, which step in the control process is represented by (**a**)?
1 determining the performance gap
2 determining goals
3 benchmarking performance
4 establishing standards.

19 In the diagram, which step in the **control process** is represented by (**b**)?
  1 determining the performance gap
  2 determining goals
  3 benchmarking performance
  4 establishing standards.

20 Thabo is the CEO of Computers Ltd, an IT company in Pretoria. Thabo uses certain control procedures to ensure that the company is progressing towards its goals and that the company's resources are being used properly and productively. He does this by means of the control process which consists of four steps. Arrange the statements below in the correct order according to the four steps of the **control process.**
  a Thabo revises some of the company's strategies in an attempt to accomplish the standards that were not met
  b Thabo establishes certain performance standards related to profitability, market share, productivity and staff development. These performance standards enable Thabo to monitor the company's strategies and goals
  c Thabo is concerned to see that sales are 10% lower than the previous year and decides to investigate why there was a deviation between the previous year and the current year
  d Thabo measures the actual performance of the company to indicate whether there are disparities between performance standards and actual performance of the company.
  1 b, d, c, a
  2 d, c, a, b
  3 c, a, b, d
  4 a, c, d, b

SUGGESTED SOLUTIONS TO THE FIRST FIVE QUESTIONS

Q	A
1	2
2	5
3	2
4	1
5	3

Operations management

Operations management involves managing the transformation processes in a business where goods are manufactured and/or services are provided. An operation is a process which transforms inputs into outputs but the term can also refer to any unfamiliar or new task that needs a transformation, such as a new set-up, re-engineering a layout, improving facilities, maintenance, or making a special batch with a unique specification.

MULTIPLE-CHOICE QUESTIONS

Easy questions

1 Arrange the **steps** for the **layout and flow of the manufacturing/service provision facility** in the correct order.
   a selecting the basic layout type
   b detail design of the layout
   c selecting of the process type.
      1 a, b, c
      2 a, c, b
      3 b, a, c
      4 b, c, a
      5 c, a, b

2 Which of the following **types of layout** form the **basic layout types** that depict the general form and arrangement of **operations facilities**?
   a fixed position layout
   b network layout
   c product layout
   d cellular layout
   e process layout.
      1 a, c, d
      2 a, b, c
      3 a, b, d, e
      4 a, c, d, e
      5 b, c, d, e

3 Arrange the **first five steps** of **quality planning and control** in the correct order.

a defining the quality characteristics of the product and service
b measuring the quality characteristics of the product and service
c setting standards for each quality characteristic of the product and service
d controlling quality against the set standards
e identifying and rectifying the causes of poor quality.
   1 b, d, e, c, a
   2 c, a, b, d, e
   3 a, b, c, d, e
   4 d, c, a, e, b
   5 e, a, b, c, d

4 Which **performance standards** are generally used to **measure operational improvement**?
   a historical standards
   b target performance standards
   c the performance standards of competitors
   d absolute performance standards
   e the performance of suppliers.
      1 a, b, c, d
      2 a, b, d, e
      3 a, c, d, e
      4 b, c, d, e
      5 a, b, c, d, e

5   Which of the following failures are **typical failures** that occur in the **operations processes**?
    a facility failures
    b design failures
    c staff failures
    d customer/client failures.
        1 a, b
        2 a, d
        3 b, c, d
        4 a, b, c, d

Moderate questions

6   A **jeweller** is an example of a ... system?
    1 project
    2 jobbing
    3 job-lot
    4 repetitive.

7   Identify the correct **operational process** used by BMW, a motor vehicle manufacturer.
    1 project processes
    2 jobbing processes
    3 batch processes
    4 mass processes.

8   Which of the following is **most** likely to be manufactured in a **jobbing process** situation?
    1 a bridge
    2 Nissan Tiida cars
    3 petrol
    4 wedding invitations.

9   A poultry farm is an example of a ... system.
    1 continuous
    2 jobbing
    3 job-lot
    4 project.

10 Hosting the 2010 FIFA World Cup is an example of a ... process.
    1 batch
    2 project
    3 jobbing
    4 mass.

11 The steel, glass and plastic used by a motor manufacturer refer to which **one** of the following **inputs** in the **transformation model**?
    1 information
    2 equipment and facilities
    3 technology
    4 material.

12 A goldsmith who manufactures jewellery is an example of a ... system/process.
    1 job-lot
    2 continuous
    3 jobbing
    4 project.

Challenging questions

13 Match the operations management guideline in Block A with the corresponding positive result in Block B.

BLOCK A	
Operations management guidelines	
a	Do things right the first time
b	Do things cost effectively
c	Do things fast
d	Change things quickly
e	Do things right every time

BLOCK B	
Positive result	
(i)	Higher quality
(ii)	Lower cost
(iii)	Shorter lead time
(iv)	Greater daptability
(v)	Lower variability

1 a (i)   b (ii)   c (iii)   d (iv)   e (v)
2 a (ii)   b (iii)   c (iv)   d (v)   e (i)
3 a (iii)   b (ii)   c (i)   d (iv)   e (v)

4 a (iv) b (i) c (ii) d (v) e (iii)
5 a (v) b (iv) c (iii) d (ii) e (i)

14 Which of the following inputs are used by Telkom in the **transformation process** to convert **inputs to outputs**?
   a material
   b clients
   c information
   d personnel
   e technology.
   1 a, b, c, d
   2 a, b, c, e
   3 b, c, d, e
   4 a, b, c, d, e

15 Abram Phenya from BMX Motors is the operational manager of the plant. Which of the following **activities** are his responsibilities?
   a to design the operations process
   b to plan and control the operations process
   c to determine the operations profit
   d to improve the operations process.
   1 a, b, c, d
   2 a, b, c
   3 a, b, d
   4 b, c, d

16 Match the following services (in Block A) with the three main categories of **operational processes** (in Block B) for service providers:

BLOCK A
Services
(a) Deloitte and Touche management services
(b) ABSA banking services
(c) The Sheraton hotel in Pretoria
(d) South African Airways
(e) Doctor John Doe, medical practitioner

BLOCK B
Operational process
(i) Service shop
(ii) Professional services
(iii) Mass services

1 (a)(i) (b)(ii) (c)(iii) (d)(i) (e)(iii)
2 (a)(ii) (b)(i) (c)(ii) (d)(ii) (e)(ii)
3 (a)(ii) (b)(i) (c)(i) (d)(iii) (e)(ii)
4 (a)(iii) (b)(ii) (c)(i) (d)(ii) (e)(i)

17 Which of the following business occupations can generally be classified as an example of **professional** services?
   a Dr John 'healing hands' McKluskery – medical doctor
   b Ms Jane 'do good' Jones – pharmacist
   c Mr John 'shaking bones' Dludlu – sangoma
   d Ms Tabang 'beauty in the eye of the beholder' Molefa – beautician
   e Ms Glona 'bean counter' Radebe – chartered accountant.
   1 a, b, c, d
   2 c, d, e
   3 a, b, c, e
   4 a, b, e

18 An **output** of a large bank is ...
   1 recordkeeping of accounts
   2 bank tellers and financial advisors
   3 accurate bank statements
   4 receipt and payment of money.

19 Circle the type of **layout** that is used for the construction site of a stadium for a mega sports event?
   1 fixed position layout
   2 line-flow layout
   3 product layout
   4 cellular layout.

20 Owing to high popularity, hotels charge tourists high rates during the holiday. During the off-season periods, hotels

offer much lower rates with the hope of attracting guests in order to fill up their capacity. What type of **capacity plan** is used here to accommodate variations in demand?

1 level capacity plan
2 chase-demand plan
3 demand management plan
4 production plan.

SUGGESTED SOLUTIONS
TO THE FIRST FIVE QUESTIONS

Q	A
1	5
2	4
3	3
4	1
5	4

Human-resources management and the SA labour legislative framework

Human-resources (HR) management entails planning, organising, leading, motivating and controlling an organisation's human resources, often viewed as a business's greatest asset.

The human-resources function has two roles:

* to increase organisational effectiveness
* to satisfy each employee's needs.

MULTIPLE-CHOICE QUESTIONS

Easy questions

1   Mary Mashego is the HR manager of Glamour, a large ladies clothing manufacturer, and one of her tasks is to do the human-resources planning for the company. What is the **first step** that Mary Mashego has to follow in the **human-resources planning process?**

1   Give a summary of the job and a brief description of each main task

2   Describe the personal qualifications an employee must possess in order to perform the duties and responsibilities

3   Describe and record information about job behaviours and activities

4   Identify the number of employees who will be needed in the future.

2   The crux of the **equity theory of motivation** is that ...

1   employees compare their efforts and rewards with other employees and are motivated by the desire to be equitably treated

2   a state of equity exists when an employee changes the person that he/she compares him/herself with and when they change their outputs

3   when outcomes are more than inputs inequity exists and the employee's motivation will be influenced only by absolute rewards

4   to produce a state of equity after equity tension has been experienced, the employee will prefer relative monetary rewards to absolute monetary rewards.

3   Sipho wants to know more about **Maslow's hierarchy of needs**. This theory assumes the following:

1   There are five main areas which should be satisfied simultaneously

2   There are three main areas of needs and the most dominant of these must be determined

3   There are five main areas and some needs must be satisfied before others can become important

4   There are three main areas which are activated by how much employees want something.

4   Which **one** of the following statements is **wrong?**

1   The selection process can vary from a short interview to an intensive assessment process

2   Intensive assessment involves psychological testing and diagnostic interviewing

3 Psychological testing cannot accurately predict which applicant will be successful

4 The selection process for lower management posts can be divided into three phases.

5 The '**shotgun' approach** to training refers to ...

1 sending as many employees as possible for training

2 using various sources (e.g. educational institutions, inhouse training programmes and professional training colleges) to present training

3 regarding any training as valuable

4 linking training initiatives with employees' career objectives.

Moderate questions

6 Lindi manages the HR department at Nyala Tours based in Mpumalanga. In anticipation for the 2010 FIFA World Cup, Lindi recognised that she will need more staff who are skilled in tour guiding and who can speak German. The prospective employees will need to have relevant knowledge about Mpumalanga's attractions, they must have skills and abilities relevant to tour guiding, and should be able to communicate well with German tourists. This **step of HR planning** is called job ...

1 analysis

2 description

3 specification

4 forecasting.

7 Ronny is a bank clerk. He works as a cashier but in the past year he has also worked in the foreign currency department, the bonds department and the savings department (job rotation). He is on a training programme to help develop bank managers. Identify the **development method** used in this scenario.

1 formal development inside the work situation

2 informal development inside the work situation

3 formal development outside the work situation

4 informal development outside the work situation.

Read the following case study and then answer question 8 that follows:

Sipho is the HR manager of a large, internationally-based corporate company. His objective for the next month is to review the motivation and management of the human resources of the company. This is a huge task and Sipho has asked some of his assistants to help him achieve this objective within the next month. Sipho asks his assistants to review all they know about motivating employees, reiterating that the motivation of employees is a complex matter.

8 Sipho suggests that they start with the basic motivation theories. He recalls that motivation theories can be divided into two groups: **content theories** and **process theories**. He explains the difference between these two groups to his team. Circle the correct explanation.

1 Content theories emphasise the things in us that motivate our behaviour, whereas process theories focus on why people choose certain behavioural options and how they evaluate their satisfaction following goal achievement

2 Process theories emphasise the things in us that motivate behaviour, whereas content theories focus on why people choose certain behavioural options and how they evaluate their satisfaction following goal achievement

3 Process theories focus more on the needs and incentives that cause behaviour, while content theories

focus on why people choose certain behavioural options and how they evaluate their satisfaction following goal achievement

4 Content theories focus on the fact that different people have different needs, goals and desires, whereas process theories focus on those expectations that will guide the actions of employees following given outcomes.

9 Which of the following are examples of **informal training within the job situation**?

a a one-day course conducted by the HR manager

b rotating an employee through different positions in a department

c a senior member of staff training a new employee to do the work

d a training program for new employees conducted by a consultant.

1 a, b, d
2 b, c
3 a, b, c
4 b, c, d

10 Computer Ltd has many applicants for the computer programming post that they had advertised in the local newspaper. Which of the following are **questions** that the HR manager should ask these applicants during the **preliminary screening phase** of the selection process?

a How often has the applicant changed jobs?

b What type of jobs did the applicant hold in the past?

c How quickly did the applicant progress?

d Does the applicant comply with the minimum requirements as given in the job specification?

1 a, b
2 a, b, c
3 b, c, d
4 a, b, c, d

11 Line managers of a company are informed that **performance appraisals** will be done throughout the year. The performance information will be used to ...

1 compile requirements for each job, provide a basis for financial rewards, and determine whether employees should be promoted

2 provide a basis for financial rewards, provide feedback to the employees on their performance, and to compile job descriptions

3 compile job specifications, compile a training and development programme, and provide feedback to the employees on their performance

4 provide a basis for financial rewards, determine whether employees should be promoted, and provide employees with feedback on their performance.

12 The HR planning process has indicated that a company does not have enough qualified workers to run the plant on a fully automated basis. One of the most important positions to fill is that of an electronic engineer. Which of the following **recruitment methods** will you recommend?

1 ask the line managers for referrals

2 place an advertisement in *The Sunday Times* to recruit suitable candidates

3 place an advertisement on the notice board of the company, as well as in the company's in-house newsletter

4 not advertise the post but visit a university nearby to recruit engineering students directly.

Challenging questions

13 **Human-resources planning** can be divided into three specific steps. Match the steps in the first block (Block A) with the corresponding description in the second block (Block B).

BLOCK A
(a) Job analysis and job description
(b) Job specification
(c) Human-resources forecasting

BLOCK B
(i) Identify the number of employees who will be needed in the future
(ii) Identify the work being done in the business at present
(iii) Identify the type of employees needed to do the work

1 (a) (i); (b) (ii); (c) (iii)
2 (a) (i); (b) (iii);(c) (ii)
3 (a) (ii); (b) (iii);(c) (i)
4 (a) (iii);(b) (ii); (c) (i)

14 Some information displayed on Hazel's salary advice (payslip) is presented in the table below.

NAME: HAZEL LINDT	DATE: 2010.05.25
Basic salary: R8 500,00	PAYE: R3 080,00
Medical aid: R1000,00	UIF: R115,00
Pension plan: R850,00	
Housing subsidy: R600,00	Bonus: R2 000,00
Leave credit: 10 days' vacation 12 days' sick leave	

Which of the following would be considered part of Hazel's **indirect compensation?**
1 leave credit, medical aid, pension plan and bonus
2 leave credit, medical aid, pension plan and housing subsidy
3 basic salary, medical aid, pension plan and housing subsidy
4 basic salary, pension plan, housing subsidy and bonus.

15 Place the steps in **human-resources planning** in the correct order.
a Identify the job currently being performed in the enterprise
b Identify the type of incumbent required to perform that job
c Identify the number of incumbents who will be required in future.
1 a, c, b
2 b, a, c
3 b, c, a
4 a, b, c
5 c, a, b

16 The receptionist was rated as 'very poor' in terms of her **friendliness**. In response, she could argue that friendliness should not be regarded as a **performance criterion** because it...
1 is not relevant to a receptionist's job
2 is not measurable
3 is not accepted by managers and employees as a performance criteria
4 does not distinguish between good and poor performers.

17 Peter is learning to be a train driver. At present he does not get a very high salary because he is still in training but he enjoys the work and does not want to do anything else. His elder brother, David, left home in Grade 10 to go and work on the mines. David hates working underground but knows that working on the mines is the most well-paid job he will be able to find, given his low level of education. **Choose the correct combination:**
1 Both Peter and David's motivation is external
2 Peter's motivation is internal and David's motivation is external
3 Peter's motivation is external and David's motivation is internal
4 Both Peter and David's motivation is internal.

18. **Productivity improvement** may be achieved in which of the following basic ways?
    a increased output being achieved with fewer inputs
    b increased output being achieved with the same inputs
    c the same output being achieved with the same input
    d a larger output being produced with more inputs but the marginal increase in output being larger than the marginal increase in inputs.
    1 a, c
    2 c, d
    3 a, b, d

Read the following case study and then answer question 19:

John is the driver of a 10 ton truck for ABC Transport. He has been working there for three years. Thabo, a driver of a 30 ton truck has only been with the company for six months and earns R1000 more than John. As John is a qualified driver, he assists Thabo in his job when he is sick or on leave. John feels that this is not fair and that he is not correctly treated. He asked for a raise once but the managing director threatened to fire him if he remained stubborn. John is a very dissatisfied worker.

19 Which **one** of the following **roles** did the HR manager neglect in this case?
    1 providing the company with well-trained and motivated employees.
    2 assisting to attain the employees' job satisfaction and self-actualisation.
    3 assisting everybody in the company to reach the company goals and personal goals
    4 managing change to the mutual advantage of individuals and groups.

20 **Vroom's expectancy theory** should be considered when motivating employees. The theory is based on four assumptions. Choose the alternative with the correct assumptions.
    1 Behaviour is a combination of forces controlled by the organisation and the environment. People compare their efforts and rewards with those of other employees in similar positions in the organisation; people have different needs, goals and desires. The tendency to act in a certain way depends on the strength of the expectation that the action will be followed by a given outcome
    2 Behaviour is a combination of forces controlled by the individual and the environment. People make decisions about their own behaviour in organisations; different people have different needs, goals and desires. The tendency to act in a certain way depends on the strength of the expectation that the action will be followed by a given outcome
    3 Behaviour is a combination of forces controlled by the individual and the environment. People make decisions about their own behaviour in organisations; people will perform better if they strive towards a definite goal. The tendency to act in a certain way depends on the strength of the expectation that the action will be followed by a given outcome
    4 Behaviour is a combination of forces controlled by the individual and the environment. People make decisions about their own behaviour in organisations; different people have different needs, goals and desires. The tendency to act in a certain way depends on the need for power.

SUGGESTED SOLUTIONS
TO THE FIRST FIVE QUESTIONS

Q	A
1	3
2	1
3	3
4	4
5	3

Marketing is one of the central activities in any business today. Marketing research provides managers and business owners alike with valuable information on potential and current customers. The marketing concept is the code that the marketing department follows in order to fulfil its tasks. In order to market a product or service to the right market, segmentation should be used. Marketers need to know how customers typically make decisions, so that possible needs can be identified and fulfilled with the use of the marketing mix. The marketing mix includes:

- product
- price
- promotion
- distribution.

MULTIPLE-CHOICE QUESTIONS

Easy questions

1 Nirvashni (a bride to be) sees an advertisement for traditional Indian bridal wear. She excitedly tells her mother about the advertisement. However, she did not pay attention to the advertisement on burial services that followed the bridal wear advertisement. Nirvashni has shown that ... plays an important role in **customer behaviour**.
   1 motivation/need
   2 attitude
   3 perception
   4 learning.

2 The marketing team of Toyota South Africa is in the process of developing a new affordable electric two-seater vehicle. The idea for the new vehicle has been developed and screened to determine its viability from a marketing and financial point of view. Unprofitable product ideas have also been eliminated. The next step in the **new product development process** would be to...

1 develop a prototype of the new electric two-seater vehicle
2 develop a marketing strategy for the electric two-seater vehicle
3 test the market's reaction to the new electric two-seater vehicle in the Johannesburg area
4 introduce the new electric two-seater vehicle to the market
5 develop a promotional campaign for the new electric two-seater vehicle.

3 The decision to give coverage of a news release in a newspaper depends on the...
   1 newspaper editor
   2 head of public relations
   3 executive manager
   4 news reporter.

4 Which one of the following is **not** a relevant factor in the choice of **packaging design**?
   1 re-usable packaging
   2 packaging materials
   3 the shape of the package
   4 packaging sizes
   5 the label that carries the brand name.

5   Cosmetic **samples** that will be distributed to consumers refer to ...
1   sales promotion
2   advertising
3   publicity
4   personal selling.

Moderate questions

*Read the following scenario and then answer
questions 6 to 8 below:*

Rebecca Molefe is the marketing manager of a
large ladies clothing enterprise called Fashion
Wear. A new range of fashionable clothing has
just been designed and after market segmentation has been done, Rebecca Molefe describes
the selected/identified market segment that the
clothes will be marketed to as follows: '*unmar-
ried, liberal women between 18 and 28 years
of age, with an income of more than R130 000
per year, and who live in the Western Cape*'.
Rebecca and her marketing team decide to
sell the new range of clothing at a high price
and to distribute it through two outlets, namely
Boutique 4U and Boutique Michelle.

6   Which of the following **segmentation
criteria** were used to identify this market
segment?
1   demographic, psychographic and
behavioural
2   geographic, demographic and
psychographic
3   demographic, behavioural and
geographic
4   psychographic, geographic and
behavioural.

7   Which type of **pricing** is Rebecca using?
1   penetration pricing
2   leader pricing
3   skimming pricing
4   bait pricing.

8   Which type of **market coverage** has
Rebecca chosen?
1   intensive
2   exclusive

3   speciality
4   selective.

9   A new jewellery store, Q Jewellery, has
recently opened in the middle of a busy
shopping centre. As the store hopes to
penetrate the market rapidly, the initial
prices of its products are quite low. Even
though the prices are rather low, the
blue and silver packaging in which the
jewellery is sold is quite unique.
Which one of the following statements would apply to Q Jewellery?
1   It sells speciality products, in family
packaging, at skimming prices
2   It sells convenience products, in speciality packaging, at leader prices
3   It sells shopping products, in speciality packaging, at market penetration
prices
4   It sells speciality products, in reusable
packaging, at bait prices.

10   A young man named Joey sees an advertisement for Heineken beer on TV. His
interpretation is that drinking Heineken
demonstrates masculinity and he goes
to the liquor store to buy a six pack of
the beer. Which **one** of the following
individual factors of **consumer behaviour** influences Joey's behaviour?
1   attitude
2   perception
3   personality
4   lifestyle.

11   Pick n Pay sponsors various educational
and charitable events. The retail group
is very visible in athletics, sponsoring
the Comrades Marathon and the Argus
Pick n Pay Cycle Tour. This is an illus-
tration of Pick n Pay adhering to the
principle of .... of the **marketing
concept.**
1   consumer orientation
2   social responsibility
3   organisational integration
4   product orientation.

12 In its promotion campaign, the Tommy
Hilfiger perfume 'True Star' featured the
well-known singer Beyoncé Knowles
using the perfume. Beyoncé is a reference person who admirers will look to
when taking consumer decisions. This
is an example of a(n) .... factor which
makes use of .... to influence consumer purchasing patterns.
1 group; reference groups
2 group; cultural group
3 group; opinion leaders
4 individual; opinion leaders.

Challenging questions
13 Marketing management has to make
decisions about certain variables, known
as marketing instruments. Which of the
following are these variables?
a raw materials
b the product itself
c the distribution of the product
d the marketing communication
methods to be used
e the value of the product to the
consumer.
1 a, b, e
2 a, c, d
3 b, c, d, e
4 b, c, e

14 Which of the following statements
concerning target market selection are
correct?
a The objectives and resources of the
enterprise have to be carefully considered before a target market can be
selected
b A market offering is developed for
each target market chosen
c Target market selection can reach
numerous individual target markets
d An enterprise does not own target
markets.
1 a, b
2 a, d
3 a, c, d

4 b, c, d
5 a, b, c, d

15 The principle of consumer orientation
entails, among other things, that the
enterprise...
a must provide the consumer with correct and sufficient information
b must always try to satisfy all of the
consumer's needs
c should satisfy the consumer only
within the limits of the profit objective
d should contribute to the welfare of
the community in which the consumers live.
1 a, b, c
2 a, c
3 b, c, d
4 c, d

16 A market segment for luxury, upmar-
ket furniture can be selected according
to various criteria. Match the criteria
in Block A with the possible variable
in Block B.

BLOCK A
Criteria
a Demographic
b Geographic
c Psychographic
d Behaviouristic

BLOCK B
Possible variable
(i) Consumers in upmarket areas of the different provinces, for example Clifton in Cape Town and Sandton in Johannesburg
(ii) Consumers with ambitious personality traits from affluent social groups
(iii) Consumers who are looking for the benefit of prestige
(iv) Consumers in the higher income bracket with a professional occupation

1 a (iv)   b (i)   c (iii)   d (ii)
2 a (ii)   b (i)   c (iv)   d (iii)
3 a (ii)   b (iv)   c (i)   d (iii)
4 a (iv)   b (i)   c (ii)   d (iii)

Read the case study below and then answer questions 17 and 18:

Maxo, a large computer company has experienced a decline in its computer sales. The company has decided to conduct a survey to determine the cause of the sales decline.

17 Arrange in the **correct order** the first five steps that Maxo should follow when conducting a survey.
    a investigating the hypotheses
    b testing the questionnaire
    c describing the problem
    d formulating probable explanations and causes
    e compiling the questionnaire.
       1 a, b, c, d, e
       2 b, d, c, a, e
       3 e, a, b, d, c
       4 c, d, a, e, b

18 Which of the following **behavioural criteria** are relevant in **market segmentation?**
    a product usage
    b brand loyalty
    c post-purchase evaluation
    d reverse price sensitivity.
       1 a, c
       2 a, b, d
       3 b, c, d
       4 a, b, c

Read the case study below and then answer question 19:

Beauty Care is a new cosmetics company situated in Gauteng. The marketing manager has decided to develop a marketing communication campaign to make consumers aware of Beauty Care's cosmetics and to persuade consumers to purchase its cosmetics. A decision has been taken to train sales representatives on the company's products. Sales representatives will be expected to visit retailers and sell directly to consumers. They will be expected to distribute samples of the cosmetics to consumers as well as dealers. A competition will also be developed where consumers will be asked to design a logo for the company. In addition to the above marketing communication activities, it was also decided that Beauty Care would be one of the sponsors of the Miss South Africa competition and that diaries with the company name on them would be distributed to as many people as possible.

19 Which of the following **marketing communication methods** does Beauty Care **not** make use of?
    a personal selling
    b direct marketing
    c advertising
    d publicity
    e sales promotion.
       1 a, b, e
       2 a, d
       3 b, c
       4 b, d, e

20 In terms of the **marketing concept** and the **principle of social responsibility**, which two of the following statements are **correct?**
    a Marketing management has a responsibility towards the community
    b It is not the responsibility of marketing management to initiate sponsorship projects
    c A sponsored event is the responsibility of the public relations department
    d A merit of the marketing concept is that it purposely exploits consumers for higher profits
    e A business is entitled to its profit to offset the risks involved in developing products.
       1 b, d
       2 a, e
       3 c, d
       4 b, c

SUGGESTED SOLUTIONS
TO THE FIRST FIVE QUESTIONS

Q	A
1	3
2	1
3	1
4	1
5	1

Financial management

Financial management is the area of a business that is concerned with planning and managing the business's funds in order to achieve its objectives. This department must aquire the necessary funds to run the business and must ensure the best use of these funds over the short and long term.

The financial management department has three main functions:
- analysing the financial position of the business
- managing the assets of the business
- managing the liabilities of the business.

MULTIPLE-CHOICE QUESTIONS

Easy questions

1 Which of the following options are correct?
   Shareholders' interest consists of:
   a owners' equity
   b long-term debt
   c preference share capital
   d net working capital.
   1 a, b, c, d
   2 a, c
   3 a, b
   4 b, c, d
   5 c, d

2 Which **one** of the following options from the **income statement** correctly completes the following statement?
   Net income (sales) less ... is gross profit.
   1 returns and cash discount
   2 cost of goods sold
   3 operating costs
   4 interest
   5 reserves.

3 The .... implies that the business must be able to capitalise on good opportunities.
   1 transaction motive

2 precautionary motive
3 speculative motive
4 profit motive.

4 Which of the following statements on **the profit objective** when **managing stock** are correct?
   The profit objective is to ...
   a keep the lowest possible supply of stock
   b keep the stock turnover as high as possible
   c keep as much stock as possible to ensure that the business is never without stock
   d ensure that production interruptions never occur.
   1 a, b
   2 a, c
   3 a, b, c
   4 a, b, d
   5 c, d

5 ... is the ability of a business to satisfy its **short-term** obligations as they become due.
   1 Solvency
   2 Liquidity
   3 Debt
   4 Profitability.

Moderate questions

You have been given the following information extracted from the balance sheet of TBS & Sons Ltd. Use this information to answer questions 6 to 8 below.

Cash and cash equivalent	R 15 000
Debtors or receivables	R250 000
Inventories	R420 000
Creditors	R120 000
Accruals	R280 000

6   The **net working capital is**... .
   1   R325 000
   2   R285 000
   3   R380 000
   4   R450 000.

7   The **current ratio is**... .
   1   2 : 1
   2   1,51 : 1
   3   1,71 : 1
   4   1,1 : 1.

8   The **acid-test ratio is** ... .
   1   1 : 1
   2   0,9 : 1
   3   1,1 : 1
   4   0,7 : 1.

Use the following information to answer questions 9 and 10 below:

Teba Ltd, a soccer ball manufacturing company, produced 2 500 units at R17 per unit. At the end of their financial year, their financial statements reflect the following costs:

Salaries	R10 000
Rent of factory	R15 000
Materials	R 7 500
Depreciation	R 5 000

9   Which one of these costs is classified as **variable cost**?
   1   salaries
   2   factory rental
   3   materials
   4   depreciation.

10 What is the **profit/loss** of Teba Ltd?
   1   R35 000
   2   R27 500
   3   R12 500
   4   R 5 000.

Study the graph below and then answer questions 11 and 12.

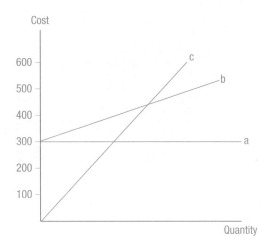

11 In the above graph, (a) represents ....
   and (b) represents ....
   1   total fixed cost, total variable cost
   2   total variable cost, total fixed cost
   3   total cost, total fixed cost
   4   total fixed cost, total cost.

12 What amount in the graph constitutes **total fixed cost**?
   1   R200
   2   R300
   3   R500
   4   R600.

Challenging questions

13 Calculate the **total present value** of the following cash flow amounts received at the end of each year. The interest rate is 10%.

Year	Cash flow
1	R3 000
2	R2 000
3	R5 000

FUTURE VALUE FACTORS			
Periods (*n*)	5%	10%	15%
1	1,0500	1,1000	1,1500
2	1,1025	1,2100	1,3225
3	1,1576	1,3310	1,5209
4	1,2155	1,4641	1,7490
5	1,2763	1,6105	2,0114

DISCOUNTING FACTORS			
Periods (*n*)	5%	10%	15%
1	0,9524	0,9091	0,8696
2	0,9070	0,8264	0,7561
3	0,8638	0,7513	0,6575
4	0,8227	0,6830	0,5718
5	0,7835	0,6209	0,4972

1 R8 137
2 R7 409
3 R7 513
4 R8 990.

14 Given the following information, which of the following calculations are correct concerning **cost-volume-profit relationships**?

Selling price per unit   = R20
Total variable costs   = R1 000
Fixed costs per unit   = R3
Total fixed costs   = R600

a Number of units sold   = 200 units
b Total profit generated   = R2 400
c Number of units to
   break even   = 50 units
d Marginal income
   per unit   = R15.

1 a, b
2 a, b, d
3 c, d
4 b, c, d
5 a, b, c, d

15 On 1 January 2006, a person deposits R3 000 in a savings account at a rate of return of 10% per annum. On 1 January 2008, he deposits another R1 000 in that account. On 31 December 2008, he closes the account and invests the total proceeds in another account on 1 January 2009 at a rate of return of 15%. How much money will he have in the account on 31 December 2010?

FUTURE VALUE FACTORS			
Periods (*n*)	5%	10%	15%
1	1,0500	1,1000	1,1500
2	1,1025	1,2100	1,3225
3	1,1576	1,3310	1,5209
4	1,2155	1,4641	1,7490
5	1,2763	1,6105	2,0114

DISCOUNTING FACTORS			
Periods (*n*)	5%	10%	15%
1	0,9524	0,9091	0,8696
2	0,9070	0,8264	0,7561
3	0,8638	0,7513	0,6575
4	0,8227	0,6830	0,5718
5	0,7835	0,6209	0,4972

1 R6 735.49
2 R6 255.42
3 R6 162.53
4 R5 723.30.

The following information was gathered by an analyst from RMB about Timbuktu Ltd. Make use of this information to answer questions 16 and 17.

CAPITAL STRUCTURE	COST
30% Equity	17%
70% Debt	12%

16 Assuming a tax rate of 35%, what is Timbuktu's **after tax cost of debt?**
1 5,00%
2 7,80%
3 11,05%
4 12,00%.

17 What is Timbuktu's **weighted average cost of capital** (WACC)?
1 10,56%
2 11,12%
3 12,50%
4 13,50%.

18 You have been given the following information about project X and project Y. The discount rate for both projects is 10%.

		Project X	Project Y
	Initial invest-ment	R100 000	R180 000
Year	Time	Net cash flow	Net cash flow
1	T=1	R20 000	R90 000
2	T=2	R30 000	R150 000
3	T=3	R50 000	R60 000
4	T=4	R10 000	R30 000

The **NPV** for project X and project Y is ....
1 −R10 000 and −R150 000
2 R86 748 and R269 484
3 R89 484 and −R13 252
4 −R12 631 and R91 347.

19 Based on your answer, it is advisable to....
1 accept both projects
2 accept project X and reject project Y
3 accept project Y and reject project X
4 reject both projects.

20 The following information is given:
Bid Best Ltd has a marginal tax rate of 30% and the following book values for its capital structure:

CAPITAL COMPONENTS	
Owners' equity	R400 000
10% preference shares	R100 000
Long-term debt [10% debentures]	R300 000

The cost of owners' equity is 15% and the cost of debentures is before tax. The **WACC** is....
1 11,7%
2 12,5%
3 7%
4 11,4%.

SUGGESTED SOLUTIONS TO THE FIRST FIVE QUESTIONS

Q	A
1	2
2	2
3	3
4	1
5	2

Purchasing and supply management

Purchasing and supply management involves selecting suppliers, determining the form that the acquired material has to take, timing purchases, determining prices and controlling quality. Essentially, purchasing management involves buying goods and services of the right quality and quantity, from the right supplier, at the right price and time. After the transformation process is complete, the goods and services have to be moved to customers.

Purchasing and supply management involves:

- obtaining materials, goods or services
- arranging how these get from suppliers to the organisation that needs them
- transportation
- warehousing
- handling materials.

MULTIPLE-CHOICE QUESTIONS

Easy questions

1 MTN uses ... as a tool for laying down standards to measure the performance of the purchasing and supply function.
   1 benchmarking
   2 decentralised practices
   3 profit-leverage effect
   4 budgets.

2 The **reasons** for **holding inventory** include:
   a continuous production
   b economical purchasing quantities
   c reduced ordering costs
   d warehouse capacity utilisation.
      1 a, c, d
      2 b, d
      3 a, b, c
      4 a, b, c, d

3 The **purchasing function** should perform which of the following **activities**?
   a choosing suppliers
   b comparing the prices with those of competitors in the same field
   c warehousing of products purchased
   d determining the quality of materials.
      1 a
      2 a, c, d
      3 a, b, c
      4 b, d

4 A ... is particularly suited to a business that comprises of **geographically dispersed** plants where purchases are made from a variety of geographically dispersed suppliers?
   1 centralised purchasing structure
   2 decentralised purchasing structure
   3 combination of centralisation and decentralisation.

5 Which one of the following is the **most important** in the purchasing of packaging **materials** for the special product lines?
   1 quality
   2 timing
   3 service
   4 price.

Moderate questions

6 You are the new purchasing and supply manager of Dairy Belle Cheese & Butter Ltd. You are requested by top management to clarify **the activities** of **purchasing and supply management** by writing a report. Which of the following issues should be included in your document?
   a selecting suppliers
   b advertising products to customers
   c expediting and receiving materials
   d controlling warehousing and inventory holding.
      1 a, b, c
      2 b, c, d
      3 a, b, d
      4 a, c, d

7 The purchasing manager of a toy company decides that when there are only 20 Snow White Barbie dolls in stock, he will order 50 new Barbie dolls. Which **inventory control system** does this refer to?
   1 cyclical ordering system
   2 just-in-time (JIT) system
   3 materials requirements planning system
   4 fixed order quantity system.

8 Which of the following statements on **purchasing planning** are correct?
   a purchasing is a service function
   b purchasing planning is subject to business planning
   c purchasing objectives are subordinate to business objectives
   d purchasing planning should be conducted in consultation with other functions.
      1 a, b
      2 b, d
      3 a, c, d
      4 b, c, d
      5 a, b, c, d

9 Which of the following are **disadvantages** of **too much inventory**?
   a operating capital is tied up
   b losses in terms of depreciation
   c more urgent orders
   d bigger insurance premiums.
      1 a, b
      2 a, b, d
      3 a, c, d
      4 c, d
      5 a, b, c, d

10 Purchasing and supply management have certain **aids** at their disposal to facilitate **executing the management tasks** of planning, organising and control. Which one of the following options lists all of these aids?
   1 benchmarks, purchasing and supply budgets, purchasing and supply policy
   2 purchasing and supply strategy, materials budget, administrative budget
   3 purchasing and supply policy, purchasing and supply budgets, financial statements
   4 benchmarks, purchasing and supply strategy, purchasing and supply budgets
   5 purchasing and supply budgets, purchasing and supply strategy, purchasing and supply policy.

11 Which one of the following statements about **productivity** is **wrong**?
   1 Productivity is the successful application of the economic principle
   2 Productivity indicates how efficiently labour, capital and other inputs are combined to produce goods and services
   3 Productivity improvement is the increase of the output-input ratio between two periods
   4 Productivity is the amount or value of goods and services produced in a period.

12 Swisschoc incurs a number of different **inventory costs**. The **opportunity costs, insurance costs and depreciation** of inventory are examples of...
1 inventory carrying costs
2 administrative costs
3 inventory ordering costs
4 inventory ordering shortage costs.

Challenging questions

13 The **inspecting material** is part of the ... phase while the **handling documentation** is part of the ... phase in the purchasing and supply cycle.
1 order; post-order
2 post-order; notification
3 notification; selection
4 post-order; selection.

14 Match the steps in the **purchasing cycle** (in Block A) with the appropriate document (in Block B) required for the step.

BLOCK A
Steps
(a) Development and description of need
(b) Issuing the order
(c) Paying for the order
(d) Closing the order

BLOCK B
Documents
(i) Cheque
(ii) Requisition
(iii) Specifications
(iv) Proof of receipt

1 (a) (i);   (b) (ii);   (c) (iii); (d) (iv)
2 (a) (iv);   (b) (i);   (c) (ii); (d) (iii)
3 (a) (iii); (b) (ii);   (c) (i);   (d) (iv)
4 (a) (ii);   (b) (iii);   (c) (iv); (d) (i)

15 Place the **last four basic steps** in the **purchasing cycle** in the correct order.
a receipt, distribution and inspection
b handling errors and discrepancies

c closing the order
d paying for the order.
1 a, b, c, d
2 a, c, b, d
3 a, b, d, c
4 b, a, c, d

16 The **steps in the purchasing cycle** can be divided into **certain phases**. Identify these phases.
a notification phase
b order phase
c post order phase
d paying phase.
1 a, b, c
2 a, b, d
3 c, d
4 a, b, c, d

17 ABC Fashions is a clothing store where materials are used on an irregular basis or acquiring materials can be planned far in advance on the basis of sales forecasts. Which of the following **inventory control systems** will be the best one to use in this enterprise?
1 the system of fixed order quantities
2 the materials requirements planning system
3 the just-in-time system
4 the quick response and automatic replenishment system
5 the cyclical ordering system.

18 Which of the following are the **main policies** that affect **the scheduling or timing** of purchases?
a scheduling purchases according to needs
b advance purchasing
c speculative purchasing
d minimum purchases.
1 a, b, c, d
2 b, c, d
3 a, c
4 d

19 Which of the following documents do other departments use to convey their requirements to the purchasing department?
a economic order quantity
b materials list
c order chart
d specification list
e requisition.
  1 a, b
  2 a, e
  3 a, b, c
  4 b, c, d
  5 b, c, d, e

20 Which of the following are **sub-policies** of the **purchasing policy**?
a a policy that deals with ethical purchasing practices
b a policy that deals with internal purchasing matters
c production policy
d supplier policy
  1 a, b, c
  2 b, c, d
  3 c, d
  4 a, b, d

SUGGESTED SOLUTIONS TO THE FIRST FIVE QUESTIONS

Q	A
1	1
2	3
3	2
4	2
5	2

The strategic-management process

The strategic-management process is a broad management approach that includes and directs management activities at all levels of the organisation. To guide the organisation in the right direction information sourced from management intelligence systems are used. This forms the focus area of this chapter.

MULTIPLE-CHOICE QUESTIONS

Easy questions

1   Which of the following statements regarding the **strategic-management** process are **correct**?
    a   It considers the opportunities and threats as well as the strengths and weaknesses of the organisation
    b   It provides direction and intent
    c   It identifies the most suitable ways to create value for shareholders
    d   Business intelligence is indispensable for the strategic process to succeed.
       1   a, b
       2   c, d
       3   a, b, c, d
       4   b, c

2   Match the **concept** in Block A with the **explanation** in Block B.

BLOCK A
Concept
a   First-line-management
b   Corporate level
c   Production efficiency
d   Business level

BLOCK B
Explanation
(i)   Creating shareholder value is a goal set at ………
(ii)   The goal at operations management level is ………
(iii) The responsibility at operations level resides with ………
(iv)   The establishment of a sustainable competitive advantage occurs at ………

1   a (i);   b (ii);   c (iii);   d (iv)
2   a (ii);   b (i);   c (iii);   d (iv)
3   a (ii);   b (iii);   c (i);   d (iv)
4   a (iii); b (i);   c (ii);   d (iv)

3   How **many** of the following statements regarding **strategic intent** and **strategic objectives** are correct?
    a   A vision statement must inspire the stakeholders
    b   A vision statement must identify with the business
    c   A vision statement must be forward looking
    d   A vision statement forms part of the strategic intent of the business
    e   A vision statement can be generic in nature

1 a, b, c, d, e
2 a, b, c, d
3 a, b, c
4 a, b

Moderate questions

4 Match the concept in Block A with the explanation in Block B.

BLOCK A	
Consistency	
a	Dynamic consistency
b	Internal consistency
c	Ensure consistency
d	External consistency

BLOCK B	
Explanation	
(i)	This is the purpose of strategic management
(ii)	Selected strategies have o be consistent with strengths and weaknesses of the business
(iii)	The consistency between the external environment and the selected strategies
(iv)	The consistency between the external environment and the selected strategies

1 a (i);   b (ii);   c (iii);   d (iv)
2 a (iii);   b (i);   c (ii);   d (iv)
3 a (iii);   b (iv);   c (i);   d (ii)
4 a (iv);   b (iii);   c (i);   d (ii)

5 Read the Standard Bank (retail division's) vision statement below and answer the question.

Vision statement of Standard Bank: 'We aspire to be a leading, emerging markets' financial services organisation.'

If the vision statement is tested against the common characteristics of a vision statement we say that:
a it is inspiring
b it must be short enough

c must be closely identified with the bank
d it contains the future direction of the bank.

How **many** of these **characteristics** are met by the Standard Bank vision statement?
1 not one
2 one
3 two
4 three
5 four.

6 Competitive intelligence helps to answer the following issues regarding the strategic-control process:
a It can predict the impact of potential catastrophic events on the chosen strategy
b It makes the organisation aware of opportunities and threats
c It can test the assumptions used to base the strategy
d It helps the organisation to scan its business environment.

How **many** of these statements are **correct**?
1 a, b, c, d
2 a, b, c
3 a, b
4 a, d
5 b, c

7 Which **one** of the following statements is **incorrect**?
1 BIS (business intelligence systems) are used to integrate different information systems
2 Data mining is not an example of a business-information management tool
3 Online analytical processing (OLAP) is helpful to view data from a data warehouse in a multi-dimensional format

4 Management dashboards is an example of an executive information system (EIS).

Challenging questions

8 Look at MTN's vision: 'MTN's vision is to be the emerging market's leading telecommunication provider. Our strategy is built on three pillars: consolidation and diversification; leveraging our footprint and intellectual capacity; and convergence and operational evolution.' How many of the following **characteristics** are included in this vision statement?
a inspiration
b conciseness
c closely identifiable with MTN
d indicates future direction.
   1 all four characteristics are covered
   2 only three characteristics are covered
   3 only two characteristics are covered
   4 only one characteristic is covered
   5 not one of the characteristics are covered

9 Match the **level of management** in Block A with the **time frame** in Block B and the **specific goal** of the business in Block C.

BLOCK A
Level of Management
Corporate
Business
Functional
Operational

BLOCK B	
Time frame	
a	Day-to-day
b	Three to five years
c	Three to five years and longer
d	One year

BLOCK C	
Time frame	
(i)	Create shareholder value
(ii)	Effective implementation of business strategy
(iii)	Production efficiency
(iv)	Creative sustainable advantage

1 Corporate: a, i
   Business: b, ii
   Functional: c, iii
   Operational: d, iv
2 Corporate: b, i
   Business: a, ii
   Functional: c, iv
   Operational: d, iii
3 Corporate: c, i
   Business: b, iv
   Functional: d, ii
   Operational: a, iii
4 Corporate: d, ii
   Business: c, iii
   Functional: a, iv
   Operational: b, i
5 Corporate: b, i
   Business: d, ii
   Functional: c, iii
   Operational: a, iv.

10 Which of the following statements are **correct**?
a Information in the public domain can provide the organisation with a sustainable competitive advantage
b Human intelligence can mostly be found inside the organisation
c Human intelligence is fully dependant on the quality of relationships with the information sources
d Human intelligence could also include 'spying' although this is frowned upon.
   1 a, b, c, d
   2 a, b, c
   3 b, c

4 b, c, d
5 a, d

SUGGESTED SOLUTIONS
TO THE FIRST FIVE QUESTIONS

Q	A
1	3
2	3
3	2
4	2
5	4